Consciousness and the Absolute
The Final Talks of Sri Nisargadatta Maharaj

Also from the Acorn Press
Books by and about Sri Nisargadatta Maharaj

I AM THAT; TALKS WITH SRI NISARGADATTA MAHA-
RAJ. Compiled and translated by Maurice Frydman; revised
and edited by Sudhakar S. Dikshit. xxii, 550 pages, illus.
Paperback.
Maharaj's unique teaching, in this compilation, has been
hailed as the direct path to the pathless goal of self-realization. The central core of master's teaching: Until man can
free himself from false identifications, from pretensions and
delusions of various kinds, he cannot come face to face with
the eternal verity that is latent within his own self. "What
the mind invents, the mind destroys. But the real is not invented and cannot be destroyed ..." says Maharaj.

SEEDS OF CONSCIOUSNESS; THE WISDOM OF SRI
NISARGADATTA MAHARAJ. Edited by Jean Dunn; intro-
duction by Ramesh S. Balsekar. 215 pages. Paperback.
(Selected talks of Maharaj from July 1979 to April 1980.)

PRIOR TO CONSCIOUSNESS; TALKS WITH SRI NISAR-
GADATTA MAHARAJ. Edited by Jean Dunn. 157 pages, illus.
Paperback. (Selected talks, 1980-81.)

EXPLORATIONS INTO THE ETERNAL: FORAYS INTO
THE TEACHING OF SRI NISARGADATTA MAHARAJ. By
Ramesh S. Balsekar. xiv, 261 pages. Paperback.

POINTERS FROM NISARGADATTA MAHARAJ. By
Ramesh S. Balsekar; edited by Sudhakar S. Dikshit. xvi,
223 pages. Paperback. "This publication is alive with the intensity and force of Nisargadatta Maharaj's spiritual realization, and the fierceness and dedication with which he
relentlessly strove to accelerate others' liberation."

Available from
The Acorn Press, P. O. Box 3279, Durham, NC 27715-3279.
Tel. (919) 471-3842. FAX (919) 477-2622

CONSCIOUSNESS AND THE ABSOLUTE

The final talks of
Sri Nisargadatta Maharaj

Edited by
Jean Dunn

THE ACORN PRESS
Durham, North Carolina

First published 1994

ISBN 0-89386-041-7
Library of Congress Catalog Card No. 94-94237

Maharaj's photographs by Jitendra Arya

Printed in the United States of America.

Acknowledgments

Sri Nisargadatta Maharaj's talks were taped by Ms. N. Vanaja, who never missed a meeting. We are all grateful to her for her dedicated service.

I was with Maharaj continuously during the time I was transcribing the talks from tapes to manuscript, and I transcribed all these tapes on a daily basis. With his blessings I came back to America on April 24, 1981, to try to get his talks published before his death. However, they were not in print until after his death.

Since Maharaj spoke only Marathi, translators were always present. Chief among them were Saumitra K. Mullarpattan, who was with Maharaj for many years; Ramesh S. Balsekar, who was with Maharaj for the last three years of his life and Damayanti Doongaji, who was a long time disciple. Our most grateful thanks go to all of them.

I am especially grateful to Marjorie Russell, for her assistance in preparing this manuscript for publication.

Abiding by the wishes of my Guru, Nisargadatta Maharaj, who wanted to publish his talks without any alterations, I have not changed the wording as translated. The manuscript has been edited for punctuation only, not for language or style. If readers have any difficulty in understanding some of the expressions, a glossary has been provided at the end.

Several of Maharaj's talks are repetitive. The explanation is that even toward the end of his life, when his body was very weak, Maharaj continued to hammer home his teachings. Nowhere is this more apparent than in his final words to us in *Consciousness and the Absolute.*

JD

Introduction

The teachings of Nisargadatta Maharaj have been published in several books using the original question-and-answer format in which the teachings were given. Maurice Frydman's translation of Maharaj's talks, *"I Am That"* and other collections which followed, including my own, have served as guideposts to Maharaj's philosophy. Many people from the West have come to follow his precepts through their reading of these collections. Now, another in the golden link of guideposts is presented here as *"Consciousness and the Absolute"*.

In this book you will find the last teachings of Sri Nisargadatta Maharaj, the final dialogues he had with the people who had come from all over the world to hear his words. These talks, coming during the last days of his life, were the culmination of the rarest teachings he had to give us; they were the summit of the heights of his wisdom.

The scene for these talks was the small upstairs room which he had built some fifty years before, for his own meditation. So many seekers had come to him for spiritual guidance over a span of forty years! Now his talks were short, terse, during the pain-filled days of the illness (cancer). It was abundantly clear that although the body was in terrible pain, he knew he was not that body. We knew his body was suffering because he told us; yet we never heard a moan or a whimper from his lips. It was awe-inspiring simply to watch him.

Maurice Frydman described this great teacher as "warm-hearted, tender, shrewdly humorous, absolutely fearless and true; inspiring, guiding and supporting all who come to him." Others have described him as a tiger. He was whatever was needed: kind, gentle, patient, abrupt, abrasive, impatient. Moods passed over him like summer breeze, barely touching him.

The force of his message resounds with his singleness of purpose: "Give up all you have read and heard and just BE. You, as the Absolute, are not this "I Amness", but presently you have to abide in "I Amness". He says it again and again. But the very repetition of his teachings is meaningful, for we have built up a hard shell around this pseudo-ego to protect it; therefore, constant hammering is needed to break this shell. The repetitious style of his teaching is part of his wisdom and teaching skill.

He taught us to find out for ourselves, to ponder his words, and ask ourselves, "Can this be true?" He said one must find out what the body is, where it came from, study it with detachment, watch it without judging. One soon sees that it is just like a robot which has been programmed by others. We are to turn within to that which lets us know that we are, to become one with that.

Abiding in the "I Amness" (or Consciousness, which is pure love), that Consciousness itself will give us all the answers. At the present time, Consciousness is what we are, not personal Consciousness, but impersonal, universal Consciousness. In course of time, the Consciousness will show us that we are not even this, but we are that Eternal Absolute, unborn, undying.

All shadings of his singular wisdom are reflected during these last, poignant conversations with those who were privileged to be in his presence.

When you read his words, may you find in them his blessings.

JEAN DUNN

May 1, 1980

Questioner: *How does a jñani see the world?*

Maharaj: A jñani is aware of the origin and the value of consciousness, this beingness, which has spontaneously dawned on him. This same consciousness plays a multitude of roles, some happy, some unhappy; but whatever the roles, the jñani is merely the seer of them. The roles have no effect on the jñani.

All your problems are body-mind problems. Even so, you cling to that body. Since you identify with the body-mind, you follow certain polite modes of expression when you talk. I do not. I might embarrass you; you may not be able to take what I say. I have no sense of propriety.

You are bound by your own concepts and notions. Actually, you love only this sense of "I"; you do everything because of this. You are not working for anybody, nor for the nation, but only for this sense of "I" which you love so much.

Q: *But I like to act; I like to work.*

M: All these activities go on, but they are only entertainment. The waking and deep sleep states come and go spontaneously. Through the sense of "I", you spontaneously feel like working. But find out if this sense of "I" is real or unreal, permanent or impermanent.

The "I" which appears is unreal. How unreal it is I have proven. The moment the "I" is proven unreal, who is it who knows that the "I" is unreal? This knowledge within you that knows the "I" is unreal, that knowledge which knows change, must itself be changeless, permanent.

You are an illusion, *Maya*, an imagination. It is only because I know that I'm unreal that I know you also are

1

unreal. It is not like this: Because I am real, you are unreal. It is like this: Because I am unreal, everything is unreal.

Consciousness depends on the body; the body depends on the essence of food. It is the Consciousness which is speaking now. If the food-essence is not present, the body cannot exist. Without the body, would I be able to talk?

Can you do anything to retain this sense of "I"? As it came spontaneously, so will it go. It will not forewarn you by announcing, "I am going tomorrow."

A doubt has arisen and you are trying to find the solution, but who is it who has this doubt? Find out for yourself.

May 10, 1980

Maharaj: How did I get to the truth that I prevail everlastingly? By meditating on the meditator, by "I Amness" merging into "I Amness". Only then did I understand what my true nature is. The great Sages meditated in the same way. Nobody had told me how to do it. I did not seek this knowledge externally. It sprouted within me.

I meditated like the Sages and saw a vision. Initially, there was space, and in the space I saw the principles embodied. Actually, they have no bodies, but in my vision they had bodies. I called them *Prakriti* and *Purusha*, the male and female aspects of cosmic consciousness.

Until the union of *Prakriti* and *Purusha*, the dynamic, all-pervading consciousness lay in a dormant state. In the union of the male and female aspects, emissions were planted in the female of these figures. When these emissions merged in the womb they started taking form. After nine months of gestation, an infant was delivered.

That consciousness which was planted in the womb was the causal body, the "*lingadeha*". In that "*lingadeha*", the knowledge "I Am" was in a dormant condition. This is what I saw in meditation.

Questioner: *How did we lose this pure consciousness state?*

M: Every being experiences the *Isvara* state, either directly or potentially, but he is so wrapped up in this objective world that he loses his identity. You must know what this "I Am" principle is. It appears spontaneously and with its appearance begins the riddle of conceptual life.

Q: *How do I start this search for my Self?*

M: Start from the very beginning. In this gross world I began with my parents, because I knew full well that my principle was already dwelling there in the collection of their bodily elements out of which I emanated. But I came to the conclusion that I could not be that principle which came from the mother's body.

There is nobody here who is 100 years old. Does that mean that 100 years ago you did not exist?

Q: *I don't know.*

M: The one who said, "I don't know" must have been there; in short, you were not like this, but you must have been something. You must comprehend this correctly. 100 years back I was not like this; so, the one pointing this out must have been there. You did, and do, exist unto eternity.

What I am expounding does not relate to worldly knowledge. You do not want to give up either worldly knowledge or so-called spiritual knowledge, and yet, through these worldly concepts, you want to understand the riddle of your existence, and that is precisely why you are not able to understand.

In truth, your state is one of Absolute bliss, not this phenomenal state. In that non-phenomenal state you are full of bliss but there is no experience of its presence. In that state there is no trace of misery or unhappiness, only unalloyed bliss. What am I talking about?

Q: *Ananda (bliss).*

M: Because you want some satisfaction according to your own concepts, you try to qualify unalloyed bliss. The term *"ananda"* has significance only when it signifies that the bodily beingness is available to experience it. When you are in deep sleep and you start to see forms, you are actually dreaming. Aren't those dream forms coming from your own beingness? Whatever you see, even in the waking state, doesn't it come from your own beingness which is dwelling within the body?

In deep sleep, consciousness was in a dormant condition; there were no bodies, no concepts, no encumbrances. Upon the arrival of this apparently wakeful state, with the arrival of the concept "I Am", the love of "I Am" woke up. That itself is *Maya*, illusion.

Q: *Does Maharaj mean that the experiencer of the three states is the Self?*

M: That is the *Saguna Brahman* state; because of your beingness the other states are. The dream world is very old, it is not new. You see old monuments in your dreams. Your beingness is very powerful.

The emergence of this beingness itself constitutes time. Everything is beingness, but I, the Absolute, am not that. In meditation, there was space, when suddenly two forms appeared out of no-form, *Prakriti* and *Purusha*, and the quintessence of these forms was the knowledge "I Am". There were no forms, then suddenly forms appeared, just as in the dream world.

You as a dreamer are sleeping on the bed, but in your dream world you see a body and you think it is you, and you are doing everything through this dream body. In that same way, bodies are created in the so-called waking state.

The *Prakriti* and *Purusha* state has no form and is eternal, having neither a beginning nor an end. But from it come the five elements, and with them, simultaneously, the body is formed at the moment that time is first experienced. This process is ever continuing, with the body-form merely indicative of the opportunity to experience time. This explanation will not reach home to everyone.

At the moment of so-called death, with what identity would you like to depart?

Q: *As Parabrahman.*

M: The Absolute, which I call *Parabrahman*, what is it like? What you are doing is multiplying words with more words, concepts with more concepts.

Q: *Maharaj must take me out of this.*

M: Can you define what you are?

Q: *I must have your blessing to understand what I am.*

M: You are very adept at word-games. While I am talking about knowledge that is beyond this phenomenal world, you are trying to understand through worldly concepts and words. Give up all these concepts and inquire into the nature of your beingness. How did you happen to be? Ponder it! The real blessing of the Guru comes when your knowledge itself sprouts inside you.

May 14, 1980

Maharaj: Doctors have diagnosed that this body has cancer. Would anyone else be as joyful as I am, with such a serious diagnosis? The world is your direct experience, your own observation. All that is happening is happening at this level, but I am not at this level. I have dissociated myself from *Sattva Guna*, beingness.

The Ultimate state in spirituality is that state where no needs are felt at any time, where nothing is useful for anything. That state is called *Nirvana*, *Nirguna*, that which is the Eternal and Ultimate Truth. The essence and sum total of this whole talk is called *Sat-guru Parabrahman*, that state in which there are no requirements.

After the dissolution of the universe, when no further vestige of creation was apparent, what remained is my perfect state. All through the creation and dissolution of the universe, I remain ever untouched. I have not expounded this part: my state never felt the creation and dissolution of the universe. I am the principle which survives all the creations, all the dissolutions. This is my state, and yours, too, but you don't realize it because you are embracing your beingness. Realizing it is only possible when one gets support from invincible faith, from that eternal *Sat-guru Parabrahman*. This state, this *Parabrahman* principle, is eternal and is also the *Sat-guru*. It is the eternal property of any devotee of a Guru.

July 29, 1980

Questioner: *Why did this consciousness arise?*

Maharaj: You are both the question and the answer. All

your questions come from your identification with the body. How can any questions relating to that which was prior to the body and consciousness be answered? There are yogis who have sat in meditation for many, many years seeking answers to this question, but even they haven't understood it. And yet you are complaining.

Q: *It is a great mystery.*

M: It's a mystery only to the ignorant. To the one not identified with the body, it is no longer a mystery.

Q: *Maharaj cannot convey it to us?*

M: I keep telling you but you don't listen.

Q: *Does Maharaj see us as individuals?*

M: There are no individuals; there are only food bodies with the knowledge "I Am". There is no difference between an ant, a human being, and *Isvara*; they are of the same quality. The body of an ant is small, an elephant's is large. The strength is different, because of size, but the life-force is the same. For knowledge the body is necessary.

Q: *How did Maharaj get the name Nisargadatta?*

M: At one time I was composing poems. Poems used to flow out of me and, in this flow, I just added Nisargadatta. I was revelling in composing poems until my Guru cautioned me, "You are enjoying composing these poems too much; give them up!"

What was he driving at? His objective was for me to merge in the Absolute state instead of revelling in my beingness.

This was the way I realized knowledge, not through mental manipulation. My Guru said, "This is so," and for me, it was finished! If you continue in the realm of intellect you will become entangled and lost in more and more concepts.

Consciousness is time flowing continuously. But I, the Absolute, will not have its company eternally because consciousness is time bound. When this beingness goes, the Absolute will not know "I Am". Appearance and disappearance, birth and death, these are the qualities of beingness; they are not your qualities. You have urinated and odor is coming from that - are you that odor?

Q: *No, I am not.*

M: This beingness is like that urine. Can you be that beingness?

Q: *Absolutely not!*

M: You require no more *sadhana*. For you, the words of the Guru are final.

October 5, 1980

Maharaj: I have no individuality. I have assumed no pose as a person. Whatever happens in the manifest consciousness happens.

People identify me with their concepts and they do what their concepts tell them. It is consciousness which is manifest, nothing else. Who is talking, who is walking, who is sitting? These are the expressions of that chemical "I Am". Are you that chemical? You talk about heaven and hell, this Mahatma or that one, but how about you? Who are you?

In meditation, one sees a lot of visions. They are in the chemical, the realm of your consciousness, are they not? All these things are connected only to that birth-chemical. You are not this chemical "I Am"!

Spiritual knowledge should not be studied; it is knowledge derived from listening. When the listener hears it, and accepts it, something clicks in him.

This "I Amness" is otherness; it is an expression of duality.

November 8, 1980

Questioner: *Why is it that we naturally seem to think of ourselves as separate individuals?*

Maharaj: Your thoughts about individuality are really not your own thoughts; they are all collective thoughts. You think that you are the one who has the thoughts; in fact thoughts arise in consciousness.

As our spiritual knowledge grows, our identification with an individual body-mind diminishes, and our consciousness expands into universal consciousness. The life force continues to act, but its thoughts and actions are no longer limited to an individual. They become the total manifestation. It is like the action of the wind - the wind doesn't blow for any particular individual, but for the total manifestation.

Q: *As an individual can we go back to the source?*

M: Not as an individual; the knowledge "I Am" must go back to its own source.

Now, consciousness has identified with a form. Later, it understands that it is not that form and goes further. In a few cases it may reach the space, and very often, there it stops. In a very few cases, it reaches its real source, beyond all conditioning.

It is difficult to give up that inclination of identifying the body as the self. I am not talking to an individual, I am talking to the consciousness. It is consciousness which must seek its source.

Out of that no-being state comes the beingness. It comes as quietly as twilight, with just a feel of "I Am" and then suddenly the space is there. In the space, movement starts with the air, the fire, the water, and the earth. All these five elements are you only. Out of your consciousness all this has happened. There is no individual. There is only you, the total functioning is you, the consciousness is you.

You are the consciousness, all the titles of the Gods are your names, but by clinging to the body you hand yourself over to time and death--you are imposing it on yourself.

I am the total universe. When I am the total universe I am in need of nothing because I am everything. But I cramped myself into a small thing, a body; I made myself a fragment and became needful. I need so many things as a body.

In the absence of a body, do you, and did you, exist? Are you, and were you, there or not? Attain that state which is and was prior to the body. Your true nature is open and free, but you cover it up, you give it various designs.

November 9, 1980

Questioner: *Should the type of dispassion which Maharaj is teaching us be taught to children?*

Maharaj: No. If that's done, they'll have no ambition to grow further; they must have certain ambitions, certain desires, for their proper growth.

The one who has fully investigated himself, the one who has come to understand, will never try to interfere in the play of consciousness. There is no creator with a vast intellect as such; all this play is going on spontaneously. There's no intellect behind it, so don't try to impose yours to bring about any change; leave it alone. Your intellect is a subsequent product of this process, so how can your intellect take charge of or even evaluate, the whole creation? Investigate your self; this is the purpose of your being.

Spirituality is nothing more than understanding this play of consciousness--try to find out what this fraud is by seeking its source.

November 12, 1980

Maharaj: The "I Amness", the manifest *Brahman*, and *Isvara* are all only one; ponder over this and realize it. This is a rare opportunity, one where all has been explained in great detail, so take full advantage of it.

You are the manifest *Brahman*. I have told you many times what your true state is, but, through force of habit, you again descend into body identification. A stage has now arrived at which you must give up this bodily identification. The bodily activities will continue until the body drops off, but you should not identify with them.

Questioner: *How are we to do this?*

M: You can watch the body, so you are not the body. You can watch the breath, so you are not the vital breath. In the same way, you are not the consciousness; but you have to become one with the consciousness. As you stabilize in the consciousness, dispassion for the body and for the expressions through the body occurs spontaneously. It is a natural renunciation, not a deliberate one.

It does not mean that you should neglect your worldly duties; carry these out with full zest.

Q: *Shouldn't we rediscover the freedom of the little baby from the body?*

M: Understand the source of child. The child is a product of the sperm of the father and the ovum of the mother. Consciousness is there in the child as it is in the parents; it is always the same consciousness whether in the child or the adult. There is only one consciousness. You must become one with and stabilize in that consciousness, then you transcend it. That consciousness is your only capital. Understand it.

To what extent do you know yourself?

Q: *I have held the feet of Sat-guru, beyond that I don't know anything.*

M: You must do that, but you should understand the meaning of "feet of *Sat-guru.*" Understand that, as movement begins with the feet, so movement begins from no-knowingness to knowingness. When the knowingness occurs, that is *Sat-guru* movement. Go to the source for that movement where the "I Amness" begins. The effort of the one who has arrested that movement will not go to waste. Holding the feet of the *Sat-guru* is the boderline between knowingness and no-knowingness.

November 17, 1980

Questioner: *Don't we have to discard all knowledge?*

Maharaj: You must have a thorough knowledge of this consciousness, and having known everything about the consciousness you come to the conclusion that it is all unreal, and then it should drop off. Having listened to these talks, sit and meditate, "That which I have heard, is it true or not?" Then you will understand that this is also to be discarded.

The principle which can pass judgement on whether the world is or is not, that principle antedates the world. That by which everything is known, whether it is or is not - who knows this?

When I say *Parabrahman*, then you say that you understand. Names are merely an instrument for communicating. Do you understand what I am driving at?

Q: *The jñani knows that this is all an illusion, that there is no path; but if, from within the illusion, one is convinced that there is a path, and there's somewhere to go, does it make sense to use techniques to get to that further illusion?*

M: Illusion - is it a word or not?

Q: *It's a word that relates to a concept.*

M: That is also a name only, is it not?

Q: *Yes.*

M: So what illusory word do you want that will satisfy you?

November 18, 1980

Maharaj: My present outlook is without limitation, total freedom.

Ultimately one must go beyond knowledge, but the knowledge must come, and knowledge can come by constant meditation. By meditating, the knowledge "I Am" gradually settles down and merges with universal knowledge, and thereby becomes totally free, like the sky, or space.

Those who come here with the idea of getting knowledge, even spiritual knowledge, come here as individuals aspiring to get something; that is the real difficulty. The seeker must disappear.

When you know your real nature the knowledge "I Am" remains, but that knowledge is unlimited. It is not possible for you to acquire knowledge, you *are* knowledge. You are what you are seeking.

Your true being exists prior to the arising of any concept. Can you, as an object, understand something that existed prior to the arising of a concept? In the absence of consciousness is there any proof of the existence of anything? Consciousness itself is mind, is thought, is all phenomena, all manifestation. Apprehending this is being dead to "I am the body" while alive. This kind of knowledge comes only in a rare case, and is a very elusive kind of knowledge where no effort is necessary; in fact, effort itself is a hindrance. It is intuitive understanding.

Questioner: *Then should all spiritual disciplines be dropped?*

M: At the highest level this is so; at the earlier levels you have to do your homework.

Those who are able intuitively to grasp this lose their interest in worldly affairs. Having lost it, what will they get? Whatever they have lost, they will have lost as an ordinary person, but what they get in return will be fit for a King. Those who have comprehended and who have reached a certain stage will not ask for anything, but everything will come to them spontaneously. There will be no wish for it; nevertheless, it will be there.

This does not happen for an individual -- it happens for the universal manifestation, or for the one who has become one with his true nature. For the jñani, only witnessing is taking place.

November 20, 1980

Maharaj: The principle which can know itself is in the organism. In a worm crawling, it is there, because the worm knows itself instinctively.

By listening to my talks you will be transformed back to your original state, prior to your birth. Right now, in spite of your present life, it will happen. My present talk is quite different now, at a higher level; therefore I do not invite anybody to listen to my present talks. I recommend that nobody should come and listen because they will develop a dispassion for their family or daily life.

Language energy and vital breath energy should merge and stabilize. Otherwise, if you allow them to go outward, they will be dissipated.

If you want peace, stabilize at that point where you started to be, stay put there. Om is the unstruck sound, the un-pronounced word.

You don't respond to my talks, you have not been able to perceive the nature of your consciousness. Consciousness is something like the drama of a play, play-acting. You are unsupported, you have no support at all. The birth, the parents, all this is illusion. Taking the body as oneself is the accident. If you don't cling to the the body as your identity, everything is all right.

When beingness forgets itself, that state is *Parabrahman*. This knowingness is not your true state, it is the outcome of the food essence body, and you, the Absolute, are not that.

November 21, 1980

Maharaj: Whatever I had thought earlier has now changed. What is happening now is that even the slightest touch of individuality has completely disappeared, and it is consciousness as such which is spontaneously experiencing. The result is total freedom. All the time there was complete conviction that it was consciousness which was experiencing; but that "I" which the consciousness was experiencing was there. Now that has totally disappeared; therefore, whatever happens in the field of consciousness, I, who am there before consciousness, am not concerned in any way. The experience is of consciousness experiencing itself.

Nevertheless, understand what consciousness is, even if consciousness is not an individual. The basis and source of consciousness is in the material. What I say is still in the conceptual world, and you need not accept it as truth. Nothing in the conceptual world is true.

Once the disease was diagnosed, the very name of the disease started various thoughts and concepts. Watching those thoughts and concepts I came to the conclusion that whatever is happening is in the consciousness. I told the consciousness, "It is you who is suffering, not I." If consciousness wants to continue to suffer, let it remain in the body. If it wants to leave the body, let it. Either way, I am not concerned.

All kinds of things were happening, thoughts and experiences, and they were credited to my account, but once I have seen what it is, all those account books have been burned and I no longer have any account.

How amusing it is to see someone who thinks of himself as an individual, who thinks of himself as a doer or achiever. Whatever is happening, and the experiencing of the happening, takes place in this consciousness when the "I Am" arises.

November 24, 1980

Questioner: *If there is no difference between what is prior to birth and what is after death there is no difference, is there any reason for attempting to learn who we are now? Isn't it all the same?*

Maharaj: The light coming from the sun and the sun itself - is there any difference?

Q: *The only difference is what happens in the middle?*

M: Whatever happens between birth and death is also an expression of the consciousness only. Even in the realm of consciousness you pass the time entertaining various concepts; what else are you doing?

Q: *Is Maharaj playing with various concepts?*

M: No. It is the consciousness, it plays by itself.

Q: *Does Maharaj's consciousness play, even though he is detached from it?*

M: Consciousness is not private property, it is universal.

Q: *Though we understand this, sometimes it seems confined to a body.*

M: You are trying to understand with the intellect; just be. When I tell you that you are that dynamic, manifest knowledge, you are everything. What else do you want?

Q: *I am aware that I came here because Maharaj gives me the mirror, but this time he is showing me that I am my own mirror.*

M: That is why you should not stay for long.

Q: *After we leave here, what are we to do?*

M: It is up to you. If you abide in consciousness everything will be happening spontaneously. If you are still at body-mind level, you will think that you are doing something. If you really abide in what I say, you become one with your Self. Then people will be serving you, they will fall at your feet. Whatever is necessary for you will happen. Activities are bound to happen. Consciousness can never remain inactive, it will always be busy -that is its nature. When you come here, you have certain expectations, certain aspirations, but after listening to my talks you lose all that.

Q: *Even when I have an intuitive understanding of this, what is this reluctance to give up all that I am not?*

M: You have not stabilized firmly in that understanding. Your conviction should be such that no question at all should arise in future about that. For example, a person is dead and has been cremated, it is all over, is there any question about that? Like that, it will be all over.

Q: *What effort do I need to make toward that?*

M: Effortlessly, just be.

When the consciousness fully understands the consciousness, will it embrace the body as itself? It is in totality; it is not going to pick out a fragment of the manifestation and say, " I am this."

The consciousness expresses itself as does a light. This five elemental play is the manifestation of consciousness, the effulgence of consciousness only. The play of the five elements will finally merge into the consciousness, because it is an outcome of the consciousness.

November 25, 1980

Maharaj: People come here and stay for days, weeks, even months. The first few days what they have heard takes root, and that is when they should leave, so that what has taken root will have time to grow and blossom. As soon as the seed takes root, they must go. What has taken root must bloom, must express itself within each heart.

Questioner: *Maharaj has said, in this respect, that the teachings were his Gurus, but the understanding was his.*

M: My Guru told me that consciousness alone is the Guru, all other developments sprouted within me. The fruit should grow on your own plant. I should not sow my understandings in you.

I have no use for traditions or traditional knowledge. If you do the slightest research on tradition you will see that it is all a concept. I am concerned with only one fact. Here I was in my wholeness, not even aware of my awareness, then suddenly this consciousness sprang up. How did it come about? That is the question which needs investigating.

One must understand how clever this fraud of *Maya* is; first it shows us our body and makes us believe that we are the body, but the body is nothing but a speck of fertilized sperm, and in that sperm the consciousness is latent. You see what a fraud it is?

The essence of the body is the essence of the foodstuff, and this consciousness lies dormant in it from the very beginning. In that state of consciousness is the entire universe. Having seen this, whoever has understood is bound to be quiet, knowing that this is only a transient happening. An enormous structure of concepts being taught to us as knowledge is based on the simple appearance of consciousness.

December 5, 1980

Maharaj: This sickness gave the confirmation that there is no personality, no individual. Sickness to whom? Sickness is part of the functioning of the entire manifest, dynamic *Chaitanya*; it is the play of consciousness. My true state is prior to this consciousness. That state does not depend on the consciousness.

There is a couplet we sing at *Bhajans*, to *Chakrapani*. *Chakrapani* means that "I Amness", the life principle, the manifest principle. It is like this cigarette lighter. The gas as such has no light, but its manifestation is the flame; it is full of light, life, energy. Even in the atom and sub-atom, that energy is there.

The functioning of consciousness takes place spontaneously, and one doesn't know what will happen. For instance, I say something and M. will translate it one way, B. will translate it another, in whichever way they have understood it. This is the way the process will go on. This *Chakrapani* is "like a flywheel," Lord Krishna said, "rotating all beings." That energy which moves all things in the waking state is latent in deep sleep. How long is one unaware of awareness? One doesn't know, but suddenly consciousness arises. Does anyone think along these lines? Is it not amazing that consciousness, which might remain latent for any length of time, suddenly arises spontaneously?

Questioner: *Is universal consciousness ever aware of itself as universal consciousness, or does it become aware only when there is a form?*

M: Awareness is not aware of its awareness. If you get too much involved in what I am saying you will throw away the books you are writing, everything.

Q: *I will finish the books, then I am finished.*

M: [To Jean Dunn] You have promised me that you will complete the books. Universal consciousness will not write the books. How will you write the books?

Q: *It will happen spontaneously.*

December 8, 1980

Maharaj: I am talking about the consciousness which works through this body at the moment, but which is not visible. This consciousness is not limited to the body but is universal consciousness; I can't speak of anything else now. A person who is already dead is not worried about anything. Whether the people like it or not doesn't matter. Perhaps you may be getting some blessings, some benefits, from listening to my talks, I don't know.

All my actions are the actions of universal consciousness appearing to work through this body. I do not remember something from the past and then act; it is all action in the now.

Questioner: *Where does consciousness come from?*

M: It never comes or goes, it just appears to have come.

Q: *Why does Maharaj know this and we do not?*

M: It is not difficult for you to know also, but with what identity are you asking?

Q: *Is it karmic, can karma be changed?*

M: It is all consciousness working, not this one or that one working; it is all consciousness.

Q: *Can Maharaj, out of compassion, give me a push into that state of universal consciousness?*

M: Yes, of course, I can do that, but you must listen to me, you must have complete faith in whatever I tell you about yourself, and you must behave accordingly.

By nature I am non-manifest, yet I am manifested, but I am really not manifested. Can you live like that, as the non-manifest?

As long as the attribute is there, the quality of the attribute, the "I Am", is there; therefore, I can speak like this. If it goes away, what happens? The sense of "I" has come and has gone, that is all, I am not going to die. One who has rejected this identity will understand.

Q: *Maharaj said that he is not going to die?*

M: How can one who is not born, die?

When people first learned about this illness, those who have affection for me came to talk to me, or wrote to me, giving advice and medicine. Whatever is to happen will happen, I have no interest. I don't have fear so I don't have to do anything. It is quite in order that those who have affection for me write and come to discuss things with me; I don't listen to them, and that is also quite in order, because I am not afraid of anything.

You are asking, "Who am I?" and you are not going to get an answer, because the one who will get the answer is false. You may have an idea, a concept, and you will think you have found yourself, but it is only a concept; you can never see your Self.

Q: *What is sat-chit-ananda?*

M: It is words. You can take it that *sat-chit-ananda* is the limit which your mind can describe of that state which cannot be described. Your true state is non-manifest; the manifestation comes and the words come. The one who experiences *sat-chit-ananda* is there before the experience.

The pictures on the following pages depict the various moods of Maharaj as he responds to his questioners in his simple room which became the place of pigrimage for seekers from countries the world over.

December 15, 1980

Maharaj: Consider the status you have reached if you are able to understand what I say, and if you have understood, there will be no status at all. Your worth cannot be measured. You have done all your homework and now your *sadhana* or spiritual practice is bearing fruit; now you are here. Let it grow in you. You don't have to go to anybody else after you leave this place; that part of the work has already been done by you. Because you are worthy of that state of realization, you are here today.

Get to know that "I Am" without words which arises in the morning. Knowing the Self, abiding in the Self-knowledge, is not a mere intellectual knowing. You must be that, and you should not move away from it. Remain firm.

Do not consult others about the advice I have given to them. Abide in what I have told only you. Kill that curiosity to know what others are told; to each seeker the appropriate advice is given. Unless you abide in your own true nature you will not be able to gauge the depth of another's nature. When you try to understand others, the Self-effulgent nature of one's Self should open up completely. You will know yourself in the process. The knowledge being expounded here you will not find in any books. Now, having given you so much, you may see me tomorrow or you may not, that is immaterial, but don't forget what I have told you about your Self.

December 18, 1980

Questioner: *This consciousness is like a screen, and I am the screen.*
Maharaj: Understand what I say without concepts; you are

adding new concepts. Now go to zero concepts. There are many spiritual seekers whose aim is to acquire sufficient merit to reach a certain place, such as Heaven or *Vaikuntha*. I have had no aims except to find out. I was not aware of my awareness, and suddenly I became conscious that I am. Where and how did this consciousness arise on me? That was my enquiry, going back to that state when the presence of phenomena was not there. That is, original knowledge of the original Self. So, I went back, tracing this original Self, and I reached a stage where I wanted to know what my state was before this consciousness arose. That is the destination which I have reached. *Brahman, Isvara,* God, all these are names given to the consciousness when it is conscious of itself. If you have properly understood this knowledge, what will be your position at the moment of so-called death? It will be watching what is happening. This consciousness gradually loses everything, and ultimately consciousness is no longer conscious of itself. That state cannot be described. It is called *Parabrahman,* the Supreme Absolute, but that is only a name for communication purposes.

This line of enquiry started when I noticed that from the moment one wakes up until one falls asleep, one is very busy doing something or other. What is it that compels us to do these things? Because of what does this go on? Then I came to the conclusion that it is my beingness, the fact that I am conscious of existing, which is working throughout the day. That was how my enquiry started.

In the body the indwelling principle is the consciousness. Abiding in the consciousness, it became all manifestation. Now transcendence of the consciousness has also occurred. With the appearance of consciousness, the Absolute knows it is, "I Am". This is the experience. There are other experiences now, in this time factor, but experiences are gradually dropping off, including this primary experience "I

Am". It is only the consciousness that is going to disappear, the Absolute is always there.

What a fall! The perfect state, caught up in these experiences, and trying to derive certain benefits out of the experiences.

Q: *Is it spontaneous?*

M: Yes. Whatever experiences were happening in this field of knowingness, the Ultimate principle got caught up in that. It accepted some experience as itself. Accepting experiences as the truth, it gets more and more involved.

December 22, 1980

Maharaj: Just now I was lying down in the waking state, but with no perceiving or receiving of any words, something like a prior-to-words state.

Now the last traces of personality or individuality have left me. Last year I used to talk to people with a certain affection, but that is not available now. My dwelling place in the grosser world is gone now; presently it is in the subtler sphere, as in space.

The effect of these talks is that you will stabilize in the very source from which the words sprout. Abiding in the dynamic, manifest consciousness is abiding in the words of the Guru. The meaning of the *mantra* I have given you is that you are the manifest, dynamic principle, not the body. When you abide in that, you become that.

People think that they are coming here of their own volition, but it is the consciousness which is bringing them here, because the consciousness wants this knowledge.

My talks are addressed to the consciousness, "You have identified with the body, but you are not the body." It is knowledge which must understand its own nature, and merge with the knowledge which is its source.

People come here and ask for blessings; they don't understand that the knowledge that one is not the body, but the consciousness within, is the blessing.

December 25, 1980

Questioner: *When we are busy with our worldly jobs, what should we keep in mind?*

Maharaj: Because the "I Am" principle is there, it is moving all over. To recognize it, you put on various uniforms in order to give it an identity, but that principle is already there, and because of that principle you are engaging in various activities. Unless you wear the uniform (the body) you will not be able to conduct any activities.

This knowledge is meant for the *Isvara* principle, which is presently caught up in the illusion that it is the body-mind. You have accepted the identity of the uniform and that identity becomes your ego.

Isvara is the manifest principle by which all activities are carried on. It has no form - the forms are given because of the five elemental play. Now, that principle gets completely lost in the uniform and is recognized by the uniform only. You have the fear of death because you fear losing your identity, the body.

Since the uniform is available to you, by all means use it, but understand that you are not the uniform.

Q: *What does one do when the uniform gets troublesome?*

M: Recede into your own Self, be one with your true Self.

This "I Amness" enjoys various experiences. It becomes a beggar or a King.

Is this body eternal? The body has been changing all during your life, which identity is you?

Q: *I identify myself with my body, I know that.*

M: Who?

Q: *I do.*

M: Give me a photograph of the meaning of that word "I". You can't. That principle has no name or form or shape. My firm conclusion is that whatever is done through the uniform is perishable, it is not going to remain. Which uniform has any permanency? Once you know that you are not the form or the name of that uniform, it is all over. Suppose you have hoarded some thousand-rupee notes and suddenly the government order comes that they are all invalidated.

Once you discard this "I Amness" uniform, what remains is the *Parabrahman*. That which is eternally current is the *Parabrahman*.

Q: *Will Maharaj help me discard my uniform?*

M: What is the need? It is not eternal, it never was.

Q: *We have not discarded ours, that is the problem.*

M: Now, tell me, when the knowingness was not there, what experiences did you have? That little touch of "I Amness" and you felt the existence of yourself and the world.

Q: *How to give up this knowingness?*

M: Where is the need? If you accept that uniform as yourself, then the question of giving it up will be there. Give up your identity with the body, try to know yourself.

It is merely knowingness, you cannot perceive that state. You come here because you are ignorant, not because you are knowledgeable. This knowledge I give is only to remove ignorance.

December 26, 1980

Maharaj: Out of what is the body created?

Questioner: *It is an expression of consciousness.*

M: Is this body not composed of the five elements? You know that you exist; does not this knowledge depend on the five elements? The consciousness cannot be known without the body. It depends on the form.

Q: *Do you mean that without the body I do not know that I am?*

M: That is correct. From your own experience, not what you have heard or read, can you know that you exist without the body?

Q: *I exist without this body.*

M: Forget about what you have read. When you did not have the experience of this body, did you have the experience of being?

Q: *My English is not very good, I cannot express it, but I know "I Am."*

M: Before you were born, could you have felt or sensed or known that you exist? A jñani is free because he sees that the body is made up of the five elements and it works according to the nature of these elements. I see that body, but I am not concerned with whatever that body does. There is nothing in it with which I can identify. The essence of the combination of the five elements is the sense of being, of existing. It has all come simultaneously, I have no part in it. Feeling that I am present depends on having a body; I am neither the body nor the conscious presence.

In this body is the subtle principle "I Am"; that principle witnesses all this. You are not the words. Words are the expression of space, they are not yours. Still further, you are not that "I Am".

Q: *What am "I" then?*

M: Who is asking?

Q: *There is nothing here, no "I"?*

M: Who is asking this?

Q: *There is a sense of something, I don't know what it is.*

M: If you feel that sense of something, can it be the truth? When this consciousness goes into oblivion, who is to say what that state is?

Q: *I don't know.*

M: Because your "I Amness" is not there, you do not know yourself. When you began knowing that you are, you did a lot of mischief, but when the "I Am" is not there, there is no question of mischief.

Q: *Is the "I Am" there all the time, as long as my body is there?*

M: The "I Am" is absent only in the state of *samadhi*, when the self merges into the Self. Otherwise, it will be there. In the state of a realized person the "I Am" is there; he just doesn't give much importance to it. A jñani is not guided by a concept.

Q: *Do we have a relationship, Maharaj, when I think I should be here with you?*

M: The very thought is the relationship.

Q: *The intensity of my longing to be here made me wonder if Maharaj thinks of his disciples?*

M: I think of them more than you know.

December 30, 1980

Questioner: *I think there should be beauty in the whole manifestation.*

Maharaj: You should not get involved in what has appeared. Take a tree - the bark, the leaves, the blossoms, the fruit, all have a different nature. If you get involved in the appearance of these, you will lose sight of the source, the tree.

Intellectually, you have understood, but you have to be one with it, you have to identify with what you have understood. Understand that the seed of this body is the sperm of the father mixed with the ovum of the mother. That is the seed for the manifestation of the phenomena, but I am not the seed, I am not the phenomena, nor am I the consciousness which is time-bound.

The names and forms which you see are consciousness only. Your consciousness is very pure and that's why you are able to judge. The *Atman* is colorless, but it is able to judge colors, etc.

Your *sadhana* is over; you have reached this place.

This knowledge is for those who have no desires. The Self-knowledge is the most precious knowledge.

To you who search for the Self I explain this type of knowledge. I lead you to a state where there is no hunger, no desire, therefore I am not inclined to invite those who are worried about their possessions and their relations to listen to my talks.

When you have knowledge you see that the consciousness "I" is all-pervasive, as long as the consciousness is there; but the witness of the consciousness has no "I Am" and that is your true, eternal nature.

"I love" gives rise to great joy, and at the same time there is nothing so miserable as "I love".

Giving up the body is a great festival for me.

What is the worth of all the activities of human beings? It is all entertainment, just to pass time. You get pleasure only when you forget yourself; in deep sleep you have forgotten yourself, that itself is joy.

It is the *Atman*, not the personality, that is drawn to spirituality.

I will not expound knowledge in the future; a few words here and there will be all.

January 3, 1981

Maharaj: Beingness has the quality to become whatever you think of. Whatever concept you feed to the consciousness, the consciousness will provide you with that. Whatever you hold on to intensely, you are bound to be that, that is the quality of your consciousness. You should never think that you are the body.

Consciousness is not the body. As a result of the body the beingness is felt, but beingness is all-pervasive.

Consciousness alone feels the expanse of consciousness, but I, the Absolute, am not that.

Whatever is known is known by consciousness, is in the field of consciousness. The consciousness and the knowledge will subside when the food body dies. The Absolute always remains. The seed of knowledge is planted in you by these talks; now you have to follow it up. You must nurse it, ruminate over it, so that the tree of knowledge will grow.

January 4, 1981

Questioner: I *was pondering what Maharaj said about all consciousness being the same this morning, and for just a few seconds, it was as if everything was one and I was behind it. Is this the aim?*

Maharaj: That is not the aim, IT IS SO. It is there and it is only because of identity with the body that what is, doesn't seem as if it is.

Please understand that there is only one thing to be understood, and that is that you are the formless, timeless unborn. It is because of your identification with the body as an entity that your consciousness, which is universal consciousness, thinks that it is dying. Nobody is dying, because nobody was born.

The millions of forms are the manifestation of consciousness. It is the millions of forms which get created and destroyed, but universal consciousness itself is unborn and undying. Just imagine if all the millions of forms which have been created were still here - how could other forms be created? It is because consciousness is unborn and undying that the millions of forms get created and destroyed; it is a continuous process. Understand that what you are is this unlimited universal consciousness. Only that in which consciousness manifests itself is limited and is created and destroyed. The total potential of consciousness remains. It is unlimited.

You are seeking knowledge from the standpoint of identification with the body and whatever can be grasped by the mind. When this body machine is there, the technique of using it is there, and that is what you are identifying with now, but it is not your true identity. You have no control over it, it has appeared and it will disappear.

I talk to you from the perspective of the universal consciousness and I know that all bodies are the essence of food and that they will vanish.

January 7, 1981

Questioner: *Every time something happens now, instead of getting involved in it, I am seeing that everything is that "I Amness". I am experiencing that.*

Maharaj: Witnessing takes place, there is nothing to be done. It is total freedom for one who does not identify with the body.

Q: *Everything is happening on its own and I have no concern with it.*

M: If that is so, it means that you have understood everything and there is no need for you to linger here any longer.

Questioner [Another person]: *It is different for me. I have to make an effort not to get involved in thoughts when I meditate.*

M: It is the nature of the life force to express itself through thoughts and words, so they will keep on coming. If you have to make an effort in the beginning not to get involved, make that effort until it becomes effortless.

Q: *Does the jñani have a mind and thoughts also?*

M: Although thoughts come and go, the jñani is not concerned. Thoughts will come in consciousness; witnessing also takes place in consciousness. You must have the conviction that you are consciousness Thereafter there is nothing for you to do; leave it to the consciousness to do what is to be done. Whatever happens, happens spontaneously.

Q: *Where is the seat of consciousness?*

M: In every particle of the juice of the body. In the scriptural books it is normally given that there are various *chakra*s. Those are available if you want to locate them like that, but according to me, it is throughout the body.

Q: *What is the difference between the body and consciousness?*

M: What is the difference between sugar and sweetness? The sweetness is there in the sugar cane juice. In the body the sweetness is the knowledge you are, the consciousness. This knowingness is due to what? What is the prerequisite for consciousness?

Q: *Is it the body?*

M: The body is necessary to sustain consciousness; for the body to be, food is necessary, is it not?

Q: Yes.

M: If the body does not remain, consciousness will not remain. In the absence of body and consciousness, what are you?

Q: *I don't know.*

M: Now you want to get some benefit, some advantage, for yourself. To whom is the benefit?

Q: *Consciousness.*

M: If you are not the body or the consciousness, then what are you? When you realize the Self-knowledge, then the self is released, liberated.

Q: *Then what?*

M: Then you know, definitely, who you are. That by which you know, you know that, also.

Q: *Is that liberation?*

M: Liberation means what? It is no more there. [Flicking his cigarette lighter on and off] This cigarette lighter is the body; the consciousness is the flame. Now it isn't there anymore; it is liberated. Where is the need to label it in the absence of consciousness?

January 8, 1981

Maharaj: Outwardly you can imitate a jñani, but the jñani has no fear.

Questioner: *He is the Ultimate?*

M: The Ultimate state is that state in which there is a total end to this body, name and form. When there is no form, shape, color or name, who is there to ask anything?

Whatever happens, you accept it based on your identity with the body, and the body is time-bound.

Q: *I have experienced that it is not being.*

M: What do you understand by the experience? What is the significance of the experience?

Q: *It is not an experience of anybody.*

M: Any experience occurs where there is a change. If there is no change, there can be no experience.

Q: *It is not an experience, it is a state of being -non-being.*

M: That which you say is and is not, is it according to words, or is it an experience? I will not play hide-and-seek with words. That which you are describing, is it an experience or just the words?

It is likely that you have been influenced by what you have read and heard and therefore what you are saying is only what you have heard. Is that right, or is what you are saying a practical experience which you have had?

Q: I said before, it is not anybody's experience.

M: First I thought I was the body, then I experienced that I was not the body but I was the consciousness, then I got the experience that this consciousness is not really me, and there is no form, no individuality, no nothing. Is that your experience?

Q: *The experience is that there is no body, nothing, that I am and I am not.*

M: What is it that is no longer there?

Q: *The consciousness of the body. Now there is no more center, thoughts don't come from the center as a body.*

M: If thoughts don't come from your center as an individual body, then how do the thoughts come? Do you now identify yourself with the thoughts? Do you think the meaning of the thoughts and you are one and the same?

Q: *No.*

M: What has really transpired? What is the change?

Q: *The change is that the center in consciousness which was there is gone, the center "I Am" is gone.*

M: Tell me something about that center.

Q: *First there was a center of identification in the body and now I don't feel that. Now there is no borderline, now there is no particular entity.*

M: "I Am" means the knowledge you are.

Q: *That is now unlimited.*

M: The knowledge "I Am" has no limitation at all?

Q: *That is right. Thank you. Now I must go.*

M: When he talks, saying "I am doing this" or "I am doing that," what he means is, I am that knowledge "I Am"; that is, consciousness. Because unless the consciousness is there, the body is not. In deep sleep we are not aware of the body, we are aware of the body only when we are awake and the consciousness is there. Therefore when I say this, I mean that it is this consciousness which I am and not the body, which comes later.

This sickness is an aspect of the consciousness and I am not the consciousness. I am not the "I Amness". Whatever sickness is there is in the domain of consciousness. With the aid of consciousness, sickness is being experienced. When I shall be totally in my Ultimate state, when this consciousness is finally extinguished, THAT is my total, perfect state.

When will I have no experience of this illness? Just as the sun sets, only when this consciousness sets will there be perfect health or no experience of this sickness. So long as the consciousness is there the sickness must be experienced. What is my pleasure or happiness? Nothing other than this knowledge "I Am", this consciousness.

Your idea of knowledge is something you can catch hold of, something you can feel and put into your pocket. This knowledge is not of that kind. When I know that I am knowledge itself, what can I hope to get?

January 9, 1981

Questioner: *What are thoughts?*

Maharaj: They are the result of previous conditioning which the mind has had.

Q: *Are the thoughts of the jñani and the ignorant one different from one another?*

M: The difference is that the jñani has divorced himself from the body-mind, the body-mind thoughts will come and go but the jñani is not concerned; whereas, the ignorant one gets involved in those thoughts and the ignorant one considers himself as a name and a form.

Q: *Should I keep in mind constantly that I am consciousness only?*

M: You are consciousness and consciousness is you and that's it; it is not necessary to always keep your attention on that fact. When you know that this is your finger, is it necessary to constantly repeat that it is your finger? What is there to be done?

Q: *When an action must be done or a choice made, how should one make the choice?*

M: Just understand that it is not your personal action or choice. Do not get involved as the doer.

Why do you get involved in all these concepts? First find out what you consider yourself to be. Are you an entity? Get that problem solved instead of getting involved in all kinds of concepts. What are you? You cannot understand with your intellect, it is beyond the grasp of the intellect.

January 11, 1981

Questioner: *The spiritual experiences which I have, are they something which should not be there? What is it?*

Maharaj: It is all entertainment. You are present here; is your body not the result of someone's entertainment? So long as you know that the experiences are only appearances in consciousness, it is all right.

Understanding is not a matter of time. If you really apperceive the truth, it is simple and quickly grasped.

The conscious presence depends on the body, and the body is nothing but the sperm and ovum, so where is this "you?" This body is like an instrument that says, "I Am", like an announcer. Presently you think that you are the body-mind, and whatever concepts you have collected are flowing out. When you begin spirituality, you reject the body-mind with "I am not that." Then you come to the "I Am" only, without words. Then you are everything, you are not confined to the body.

Because of the instrument of the body, that feeling of consciousness is there and I, the Absolute, am not that.

Having stabilized in the consciousness, the next step is to be in a position to observe the consciousness, and all the play that is happening in the consciousness, just to understand. Attachment to the body and to the consciousness is very strong, to get rid of it is very difficult.

The birth principle, the chemical around which the body formation takes place, has no form or design and actually didn't exist. That non-existing thing suddenly came into existence. What is the validity of its existence? It is an apparition only, it can't be the truth. That's why I dare talk like this. This is a big hoax, a big fraud, created out of nothingness. Can you create something out of nothing?

Whatever I said is securely planted in that birth principle of yours, you cannot extract it. In due course it will proliferate into knowledge.

I don't want life, even for a moment, but in that momentary life there are so many lives.

I am not afraid of death. With death the imperfection is removed. Consciousness, the stigma of imperfection is gone. What remains is total perfection.

There is no guarantee that I will meet you tomorrow, but the reality is that there is no separation at all between you and me, because we are one. Do not imagine any separation.

January 12, 1981

Maharaj: [Referring to his lighter] The flame will last as long as the fuel is there. Is there any question of emancipation or awakening for that flame? The body and consciousness, which come into being because of the five elements, can there be any emancipation for them? The One who is prior to the appearance of the elements is always there.

What you are doing is using your mind and intellect, but what I say is not based on the intellect, but rather on whatever comes up spontaneously in consciousness. You try to fix that knowledge which springs spontaneously from consciousness into the structure of concepts you have built out of the mind and intellect. This can never happen.

Questioner: *Why do I feel such satisfaction here in Maharaj's presence?*

M: Because that need which arises in consciousness and brings you here is satisfied.

Some people come here for knowledge. I talk because the words naturally come out. There is no intention behind my talks that you should get knowledge. Others come here because they are in difficulties. I make no determination that those difficulties should go away, but the fact remains that in many cases they do go away. I merely sit here, people come and go, I am not concerned. They come here from long distances because the consciousness feels the need to come here. The individual doesn't come here because of an intellectual decision to come here. Consciousness takes him by the ear and brings him here. My next-door neighbors don't come but people from all corners of the world come here with a sense of urgency. Why?

Q: *The first time I came here, Maharaj told me that my "I Amness" was a food product, and that Lord Krishna's consciousness was the same as a donkey's consciousness. I tried to get a reservation out of Bombay that day, but I couldn't get one for a week, and I had to stay.*

M: Many talented and well-known people have come here, but they come with great humility. Is there anyone of them who has knowledge about himself?

Q: *I am practicing nama-japa, is that all right?*

M: Recite the sacred name, that is all right, but the important thing is to recognize and understand what is the presiding principle by which you know you are and by which you perceive everything else. You must look at yourself, get to know yourself. The riddle of spirituality cannot be solved by your intellect. At the most, your intellect can provide you with livelihood.

Whatever you try to become, that is not you. Before the words come out, before you say "I Am", that is you. You must be concerned only with yourself. Don't worry about anybody else. What are you?

January 14, 1981

Maharaj: The Ultimate state is that state in which nothing exists, neither I, nor you, nor manifestation.

Questioner: *Can Maharaj describe the Ultimate state?*

M: Can I cut up my sleep and make a design of it? Disassociate yourself from your body and tell me something about that. Can you describe it? My talks are not meant for normal human beings. The normal person's field of understanding does not go beyond his own body.

The one who identifies with the body is the consciousness itself. It mistakenly assumes that it is the body and behaves as if its unlimited potential has been limited by this one single phenomenon. Therefore, with this identification, whatever behavior the consciousness adopts will be limited by the body.

The one who understands this ultimate meaning of life gets disassociated from the body and a transformation takes place. The consciousness is universal, universal like the day, universal like the night. To that principle you cannot give a name or a title. Who is the one who knows that there was no day, no night, the consciousness was not there? Day and night, remembering and forgetting, the waking state and the deep sleep state, are they one and the same thing or are they separate?

The capacity of consciousness is something astounding. I didn't know I was, and then suddenly I knew "I Am". This "I Amness" is the power of *Maya*.

Q: *Is the desire to be free wrong?*

M: There is nothing happening - nobody is bound - therefore there is no question of liberation. It is only when one thinks of himself as an individual that he thinks of bondage and liberation.

Whatever concepts you have collected in this world are totally useless. Understand that the total manifestation is the child of a barren woman, but having understood this, give full attention to your work, and let that work be done as efficiently as possible. Take good care of this work that you do in the world because it is an orphan!

January 17, 1981

Questioner: *In consciousness is there doership and also witnessing?*

Maharaj: Everything is in the realm of consciousness.

Q: *Are all the actions in the world being done through consciousness? The movement of the five elements also?*

M: The sum total of the five elements is consciousness.

Q: *It's beautiful to praise this consciousness by consciousness, no?*

M: Oh, yes. Whatever you are, only you know. In the body is only the knowledge, no person. For practical purposes you use various names.

Q: *In the body, why is this consciousness saying, "I," "You," etc.?*

M: Consciousness is one, but it manifests into many, so for practical purposes you say "I," "You,", etc.

Q: *My consciousness is due to this body, sustained by this body, not other bodies.*

M: In your consciousness all the bodies are there.

Q: *Maharaj said that I am not in the body, that the body is in me.*

M: If you are an author, a number of books are potentially in your pen. Since when did you realize that you are?

Q: *When the body and consciousness appeared.*

M: The sum total of my spirituality now is nothing, even that word "nothing" is not there, so there is no spirituality left.

Suppose I do not like my body, or even the vital breath, what can I do - the body is there, vital breath is there, and therefore this "I Amness" is there. They are functioning by themselves, why should I worry about it? It is having its play, let it have it. So long as that knowingness, "I Amness", is there that attraction will be there for others. The knowingness is the outcome of the food body; when this body is consumed, where is that "I Amness"?

There is no such thing as spirituality; whatever is, is only this worldly life, in the five-elemental play. You are nothing better than vegetation. Just as grass is growing, human beings are growing. Will anybody accept this? Birth is a material aspect. If you are yourself alone, that state will not be felt; but if there is a foreign element, only then the suffering starts. On you, the original, this foreign element is imposed, that is why it is suffering.

You will not enquire into what you are. Because you are intellectuals, you will prepare delicacies out of your intellect and you will go on eating that. Even in spirituality you employ your intellect, you prepare so many delicacies out of your concepts and you relish them.

Take a hint from what I have said. That you experience the world at all is the result of somebody's fun; now it has become the source of misery.

Q: *Is it possible to be in a wordless state?*

M: Can you live without words? Words are very necessary.

Q: *We are prisoners of our own concepts.*

M: Just enquire into that birth principle. You are; because you are, the father and mother are. It's a simultaneous happening. Because of their action you are, and (at the same time) you have parents. Without their bodies what are they? Try to understand what they could be without their bodies. Ignore that action because of which you are; and then try to recognize what the parents are. As a result of these two presences, there is a third presence, "I Am". Now will you clear out those concepts of yours about parents?

January 20, 1981

Maharaj: Earlier the knowledge used to overwhelm me , and I would to invite people to listen to the talks, but that time is gone now. Now, I don't encourage people, I don't keep people here for very long. I give them a dose of knowledge and send them away.

It is most incredible in the guise of that little so-called birth, everything has happened. Not only the "I Amness", but the whole manifest world has appeared. Is it believable? Actually I am not, but I feel that I am because of the incident of that birth.

When you get this knowledge you will realize that knowledge of this world and consciousness are not even worth your spit. You can spit it out; it will be unworthy. I appeal to you with my folded hands, don't get into this spirituality. Whatever knowledge and concepts you are having, only that final spark is to be applied. You have everything, the raw material is already with you, the symbol of birth and death is already removed.

The factual state of affairs is open, very clear, but nobody wants to look at it.

Translator: He has preference for simple devotion to God. In people with devotion, even with limited intellect, the intellect is not making mischief, as it is here.

M: This is the place where the intellect gets annihilated.

I was created and possessed by the five-elemental ghost, but having stabilized in the *Parabrahman*, I know what it is and I am out of it.

Now, just see how I am possessed by these elemental essences. I am addicted to chewing tobacco; despite the advice of doctors not to do it, I am still doing it. That is because I am possessed by the essence of these elements.

Space is indicative of the world, in that space the world is. Space is like an incipient world. The world is not there, but the material of the world is there. From there I start feeling "I Am". With air the movement is there, with fire the heat, with water all seeds and everything else, and because of water the taste is there.

But you are dispossessed of these elements because of the Satguru. Satguru (*Parabrahman*) is all love for no-knowingness.Because of your association with this Satguru, it means illumination for you.

I don't feel like talking at all, I want to go into a sort of silence. My present talks, if they are really understood, require no more discipline or *sadhana*. They should click right there and then.

Q: *At one time, there were a number of saints of the highest order. Why was it, that suddenly there were so many saints at that period?"*

M: At that time the devotion was so strong that the very object of meditation would take a complete shape in front of the meditator. Because of that devotional state, the whole atmosphere was imbued with that devotion, now it is only with the intellect. People are not going to accept anything blindly , because their intellect has become more subtle, like space. They are going to pick and choose, to analyze everything.

January 24, 1981

Maharaj: Listen to what I am saying, but do not expect to benefit in any way by what you hear, because to benefit there must be an entity, and there is no entity.

Since I have had this disease there has been a slight change in the way I look at things. Earlier, I had felt that there was a slight touch of individuality, to the extent that I felt that this universal consciousness was acting through a particular form. Now there is not the slightest touch of any individual form nor functioning. There is now cognition of total functioning as such, but even that will last only so long as the body lasts. In that body there is consciousness, and both are material. In all this there is no question of any entity cognizing anything as separate. Instead, there is total functioning through various millions of forms. I have identified the disease with the total consciousness.

Questioner: *What remains when consciousness goes?*

M: Nothing phenomenal remains. The present talks are the culmination, or termination, of spiritual understanding. The more the physical pain is observed, the more it is being realized that everything is illusory.

Q: *Maharaj has reached the destination, we have not.*

M: There was a house, and in the house there was a person; now the person is gone and the house is demolished. The sum total is, whatever experiences you have, whether for a day or for years, it is all illusion. The experiences begin with knowingness.

What is the most ingrained habit you have? It is to say "I Am". This is the root habit. Words and experiences are unworthy of you. This habit of experiencing will not go until you realize that all this domain of the five elements, and the experiences in the five elements, are unreal. This "I Amness" is itself unreal.

January 29, 1981

Maharaj: You must give up identity with the body. Abidance in that knowledge "I Am" which does not identify with the body-mind is the spiritual light. Self-love and "I

Am" without words are the same. The sicknesses may come and go, but the Self-love does not go.

Questioner: *The realization of Self does not come.*

M: Who says that? Without the knowingness who could say anything?

Q: *Knowingness must exist because there is something to be known.*

M: You have come here with the idea that you are full of knowledge, full of wisdom; so what is your idea of knowledge? You are very seasoned, having roamed about in all corners of the world.

Q: *I know that I am not full of knowledge.*

M: Why do you tell a lie?

Q: *The books speak of that Ultimate joy and fulfillment which is the result of knowledge.*

M: You are not going to meet it because you are it. Would you go out to meet your Self?

Q: *No, I come here.*

M: Before you knew you were, did you have knowledge or ignorance? In the absence of consciousness, who could say "I Am"? [Long silence].
You have all gone into quietude.

Q: *Every thought, every feeling in consciousness, is changing all the time. I cannot be the changing, I am the changeless consciousness which enables thoughts to pass.. That is how I understand it. Is it right?*

M: How deluded you are!

Q: *What I am trying to do is to stop identification with the thoughts and feelings and not be possessed by them, as I use them as pointers to the highest consciousness.*

M: Then why do you talk? The pointers of your feelings and your thoughts are your Self and that is consciousness, so consciousness and your Self are one.

Q: *I want to get away from the pain.*

M: The mind is deluding you, is cheating you.

Q: *So I am the pain and I should be happy to be the pain?*

M: Focus your attention on you-are-the-happiness, then the pain will diminish. You assume that you have knowledge. You have developed a pride that you have knowledge, so for testing yourself you have come here.

Q: *I cannot help my pain by repeating that "I-am-happiness". Maharaj speaks from his level. I haven't got that highest happiness to diminish the pain.*

M: That is because you are embracing your body as your Self.

Q: *Exactly. That is why I am using a trick to escape that.*

M: Very good. In the later stages this consciousness is itself the pain. Until you recognize and completely identify yourself with the knowledge "I Am", you will identify with the body. That knowledge "I Am", you do not know her. Some others here have no pride that they are knowledgeable; you alone are claiming all the knowledge and pride. Now, how many more days are you going to visit this place?

Q: *Until the 7th.*

M: You have been given answers to your questions, why should you return?

Q: *Then these others do not have the knowledge, and that's why they can come back?*

M: You speak for yourself! Other people may be more knowledgeable than you, why do you equate them with you? You have committed a grave offense by equating these people with the level of your wisdom. Take care of yourself, don't worry about others. How dare you bother about others when you do not fully know yourself?

Q: *There is some link which binds us together.*

M: Never criticize others.

January 30, 1981 A.M.

Maharaj: Just as a person continues going to work every day because he wants to receive his wages, so you keep coming here because you want to gain knowledge. Once you have this knowledge, there is no need for you to stay any longer.

Until you get the knowledge, you don't want to leave; nevertheless, the only ones who should stay are those who feel a great urgency to know. [Maharaj sends some more people away.]

I do not want casual seekers to stay here anymore. The only ones who should stay now are those who have a real anxiety about progressing spiritually, those who are earnest seekers.

If you are an earnest seeker, you should accept my words as the truth or you should leave, as I do not want merely to entertain you. And what am I telling you? You are not the body. You are the conscious presence. Accept it and you can forget it.

In future, I will not be able to go into the problems of each one of you. I will simply tell you, "This is false," or, "This is the truth." You can accept what I say, or you can leave.

Questioner: *I don't have the capacity to accept what Maharaj has given me.*

M: If you don't think you have the capacity, then you can go elsewhere. I am not concerned with any state which is temporary. This consciousness state is not of my choosing. The sooner it goes the better. Once it is known what is temporary and what one's original state is, no further knowledge is needed.

As soon as consciousness stirred, space and time came. It has a time limit. In this space-time everyone suffers, so why should I accept this suffering as something unique? I was always in that blissful, complete, total state; suddenly I am in this imperfect state. Those who have apperceived my knowledge will not fall a prey to the logic or spirituality expounded by others. I dare to say to any scholar who considers himself full of wisdom, that when he was being born I was watching his birth from a corner. Would you accept this?

Q: *Yes. Why did consciousness arise at all?*

M: Hang on to this consciousness which has come and it will explain why it arose without cause. No one else can explain to you why and how it arose.

It is the manifest consciousness which is continuously talking, I am not talking. How does the language emerge? Is it because of your efforts?

If you grasp the essence of the talks which I am giving, you will illuminate the world. Those people who run about from place to place aimlessly will gather nothing. What is that you are after?

Eknath, a country sage who has written wonderful poems, said, "I am stung by a scorpion!" What is that sting? It is the consciousness. This knowingness is the scorpion which is giving me all the pain in the form of various experiences and concepts.

I am telling you with the authority of a jñani, everything is unreal. This is all the play due to your consciousness, and your consciousness is due to the food essence body.

Q: *I am grateful to my body which has brought me here.*

M: You have come here just to commit suicide.

January 30, 1981 P.M.

Maharaj: A real spiritual seeker ponders over these things all the time. When I have no body, what am I? What is the Ultimate Reality?

The Absolute state cannot be explained by words. Words are only pointers. You are that absolute, unchanging. Consciousness, or the knowingness, is homogeneous and one only. When you are in that state of consciousness, it is all one, all the same, only the expressions are different.

Everything which gets consumed, exhausted, is unreal. Your knowingness will, in due course, be consumed, will disappear, so it cannot be real; but you can't just dismiss it, you must understand it fully.

Presently there are an infinite number of items in your associations with this world because you have the association of the vital breath. Suppose that vital breath goes. What will happen then to all your associations with the world?

This knowledge which has been expounded will not go to waste, many people have taken advantage of it. The time will come when they will be enlightened also and then they will expound knowledge.

A jñani's state remains the same with or without the body.

You should meditate, you should not lose what you have learned.

When one disidentifies with the body, one transcends not only the body but consciousness as well.since consciousness is a product of the body. The consciousness no longer says, "I Am", "I Am".

January 31, 1981

Maharaj: I deal with only two things:. What is your identity, and what is your conviction about what you are?. These questions cannot be discussed with everyone. I can speak of them only with those of you who are in earnest. There are those who have a lot of wisdom but have not solved the riddle of "I Amness".

Questioner: *Scientists have discovered, in the last ten years, that if they don't observe the reactions of the atomic particles, the reactions remain as they are. If they do observe those reactions, there is a change. The very act of observing causes a change in that which is observed.*

M: The observer is also changing. What is being observed brings about a change in the observer, and unless that change is brought about in the observer, the observer cannot observe the object; therefore, one can never get to the depth of spirituality.

When you are cognizing something as an individual, where do you place yourself? Consciousness is that which is cognizing, the cognition, and that which is being cognized.

You are only scratching the surface. It can't do you any good at all. What you hear must enter you like an arrow and hit something deep within you.There must be an internal reaction; without the reaction what you hear won't do you any good. You should know it when the arrow reaches its mark.

February 5, 1981

Questioner: *It is very difficult to give up this attraction to the bodily identity.*

Maharaj: You have to find out what this body is, then the job is done. Initially, the body is very minute. The consciousness appears in the body, and then the tiny body changes into a large one.

That causal body, which is very minute, needs to be known. By meditation you can know it. The quality of that causal body takes on the appearance of the consciousness and the form. In this world there are many species, in all sizes; initially what was the size of each variety?

At the point where you first feel knowingness, consciousness is not static; it is a continuous state, just like a wheel moving. The center of the wheel, the axle, is not moving. As you proceed from the center of the axle outwardly, the movement increases, does it not? Similarly, the beginning of consciousness is like the center of a wheel; that point is steady, constant. In a human being that is the most constant principle. Since the day I was born until I am dead, that consciousness principle is there at that center. As you merge into the world, the movement increases. Watch that center point, watch that movement of consciousness. *Chaitanya* and *Chetana,* that central, stationary point of the wheel watches the movement of consciousness. The one that observes the movement is almost stationary.

To bring about the actions of the world -- the movement -- consciousness must descend. If there is no consciousness, there is no worldly movement.

Similarly, you must become stabilized in a more stationary position, near the center. When you leave that center point, the movement takes over.

February 7, 1981

Questioner: *I am becoming more aware of my "I Amness" as a product of the food body.*

Maharaj: You must be that principle prior to the emanation of the word "I". Suppose I get a prick here - that principle prior to the emanation of words knows there was a prick. Prior to words and feelings, you are.

Q: *How is it possible to know and feel that Absolute?*

M: This knowingness, or understanding, is in the realm of consciousness. Whatever you say that you know and feel is consciousness only. The Absolute is beyond this.

Q: *In practice, how can we go further?*

M: Deal with the consciousness only, get to know it thoroughly. That is all that can be done. Later on, everything happens spontaneously, doership goes.

Know the inside-out of consciousness and recognize it as useless; it is a fraud. When you transcend it, you will say, "I can manage without this. This is imperfect! Therefore, meditate in order to know the consciousness.

Q: *I have never been able to meditate.*

M: When you were unaware of this message of "I Am", how did you function? The questions I put, nobody can answer. All of you great scholars, people with a lot of knowledge, have gone into quietude.

Q: *My questions are answered.*

M: When your problems are solved, you are also solved. I want you to dwell on that borderline of consciousness, no-consciousness.

February 8, 1981

Questioner: *Sometimes I have a feeling of mindlessness I feel that only I exist. There is only one thing in the world. I don't have to do anything. I simply exist.*

Maharaj: That state of being is common to all, that is the message "I Am" without words.

Q: *Is it possible to remain stable?*

M: Change is only in the mind-flow. All the studies you are doing are in the realm of the mind-flow. The sense of "I Am" is present because of your birth, through which you encounter many thoughts and concepts, always changing. Presently the message "I Am" is constant.

Q: *How can one be in that no-mind state?*

M: Prior to your birth and receiving the message "I Am", what were you?

Q: *That is a mystery.*

M: It is open, very clear, but still it is a mystery. Subsequent to that "I Am" and body-mind, and in the realm of the mind, there occurs what you call spiritual seeking, or spiritual knowledge. This is nonsense. In due course this message "I Am" will disappear.

Q: *How can you say that? What about rebirth?*

M: There is no rebirth. In the case of a jñani, the disappearance of the "I Am" will be termed as Niruta, free from the "I Am". In the case of an ordinary person, involved in mind, the disappearance of the message "I Am" will be expressed as "the person is dead and has taken another birth." You can never undertake studies about that no-message state; you are making studies in the mind zone.

Q: *So the witnessing is only possible when there are modifications of the mind?*

M: Witnessing *happens*. Remember one thing, I am addressing my talk to the message "I Am".

Q: *How can I communicate with the "I Am", how can I listen?*

M: Listening will come spontaneously--just as you wake up spontaneously and fall asleep spontaneously. Don't make any effort.

I did not extract my beingness from "there" and insert it into "here". It is happening spontaneously, and therefore I am experiencing it. During these talks you have gotten very angry; this is in the zone of mind modifications - it is not a reflection of your consciousness. The one who understands that anger is the message "I Am". All your spiritual studies are conducted with your identification with the body-mind.

Q: *I think so, yes.*

M: Unless you identify correctly who you are, how can you identify others correctly? Recognize your real Self.

Q: *How shall I start?*

M: Faith in God is one of the *sadhanas*. The firm faith in the Self is not a *sadhana*, it is abidance.

Q: I *believe in God, or I do not believe in God--are these beliefs the same?*

M: Who is saying this? What you say will be correct only when you have the conviction that you and God are one, then you will recognize that there cannot be a God without you. To know yourself is the real knowledge, but you cannot LOOK at yourself, you can only ABIDE in your Self. Give up your attachment to mind modifications.

Q: *Sometimes it does happen. How can I transcend the mind?*

M: Understand that you have no connection with this mind-flow; you are apart from it. Be watchful, be alert. A century ago, were you possessed by these mind-modifications?

Q: *No.*

M: Remain exactly like that.

Q: *How can I remain in the "I Am"?*

M: It is a stupid question. You are ALREADY that. Are you not already the "I Amness"?

Q: I *can't be free from that?*

M: A jñani has transcended the "I Amness" and only witnesses it.

Q: *What kind of rule should a man choose for conducting himself in life?*

M: This question emanates from your concepts. Throw out your concepts. In the course of your study of spirituality, you have acquired many concepts which you call that knowledge. Do you want me to be embroiled in your concepts?

That thought-flow is always there, except in deep sleep. Even for a jñani, the thought-flow is present but the thought has changed.

Most people are carried away by the thought-flow, but a rare person turns around, goes to the source and departs from the track of that original thought-flow, saying, "It is not mine, not my affair. This 'I Amness' is the product of objective material, it is not me. I am out of it."

The statements which come out of here will stick to you, and with that sticking, your spiritual job will be done. When you do anything it is for "me", but there is a limit to which that can go, isn't there?

Q: *The needs are limitless.*   LIFE, LIBERTY +

M: I meet many people who, in the pursuit of happiness, are always miserable. Rarely do I encounter someone who says "I am content."

February 9, 1981

Maharaj: My present state is such that this consciousness and all this physical suffering are unbearable. I am prepared to dispose of it right now; this is the state of affairs. Nevertheless, people come here and these talks emanate out of the consciousness. I am addressing you as consciousness; you are the Godly consciousness. I am not concerned with your bodily affairs. But you listen from the body-mind standpoint; it is quite natural.

I am telling you about the consciousness. In my true state, if I had been aware of consciousness at the moment the body formation was taking place, I would have rejected it. But at that highest state such knowledge is not there and this body formation and consciousness are both spontaneous.

Questioner: *Maharaj, will you please explain how we can dive further into that consciousness?*

M: How long have you been following spirituality?

Q: *For the last ten years.*

M: Who were your guides or Gurus?

Q: *Mostly I was reading. I had a Guru in Delhi.*

M: Who is employing the body and the name given to it?

Q: *That is what I want to discover.*

M: You need not go in search of it. It will be spontaneous, but you have to wait. I had to wait such a long time to meet you.

Q: *I will wait.*

M: Now, understand the subtle difference, what are you and what do you understand to be you? The body is not you, the name is not you. The body is the food you have consumed, the taste of it is the knowledge "I Am". That is Self, the feeling "I Am", that is the love to be.

How amazing, how incredible, it has no name, but you give many names to it. It is the Self, the love to be. That love to be is all-pervading.

Heaven, hell, countries, houses, these are all concepts. There were rock and earth, a concept was employed and buildings were built. Before you conceptualize anything, you are, even before the knowingness, you are.

You have only to apperceive this knowingness, the love to be, the Self.

Who will be listening to such dialogues? Only the Self in the body has the urge to understand. People hasten to this place, travelling from distant countries, leaving their families for the time being, because the Self wants to know itself.

February 11, 1981

Maharaj: I studied the five-jeweled ornament, I have understood. It was a very precious gem, and the ultimate product was that diadem. I have understood the value of that, but I am not that.

The five gems are the five elemental body and consciousness, which I considered myself to be. It is very precious because it has the value of the cosmos. I recognize it, and in the process of recognition, I know that I am not that.

Now I rarely speak, and when I speak, rarely does anyone understand. You might collect a lot of words, but will they remain with you? You are bereft of words and the meaning of words, you are not a personality. That birth principle which gives rise to the consciousness is not conditioned; it has come spontaneously and manifests as consciousness.

How caught up you are with the world! Until yesterday you did not have knowledge of your existence, and today you are loquacious; you are speaking so loudly, and you claim that you are *Brahman.*

Questioner: *I know that I have to understand all this play of consciousness and conclude that this is like the child of a barren woman.*

M: How are you going to catch that child of a barren woman? Just be in your beingness.

February 12, 1981

Maharaj: Nothing in the world is of any use to me. That very identity with which you try to understand everything is unreal. Daily you have to convince yourself about yourself. You have to carry out your life, first of all assuring yourself that you are. Nothing has happened except the knowingness, only a pin-prick of knowingness against the background of your innate nature of no-knowingness, and this is of no help at all.

I don't have any identity arising out of consciousness.

Presently this body is undergoing a lot of agony: dizziness, pain; all these things are happening at the physical level. In spite of this state, the talk comes out inspiringly. What permits that? It is the *guna*, the beingness. That beingness not only experiences your visits here, but it also experiences various changes and transformations in this body and in the world.

Sometimes I experience the state of lying in some rubbish, and other times I experience that people are worshipping me. But that is all in the realm of consciousness. I realize this is all the outcome of that birth principle "I Am".

Will the space and the stars feel unhappy about the dirt in the world? It is part of the game in that universal space. Consciousness is subtler than space. You are bent on having knowledge at the most mundane level, but whatever knowledge you collect is bound to disappear.

There is only one truth in the world, and that is that everything is unreal. I am the Unmanifested talking through the Manifest. When the body, the mind, the vital breath drop off, nothing happens; only I, the Absolute, prevail always. No knowledge is called for to understand this truth, because that knowledge is innate.

What you have learned here will be your guide. The sprouting will take place.

February 13, 1981

Questioner: *I have so many questions to ask that it is chaotic.*

Maharaj: Your questions are regarding the concepts of others. Ask questions only regarding yourself.

Q: *I don't know my Self, how can I reach that point, how can I come to that?*

M: The fact that you do not know your Self is very appropriate; you are not the body, nor the name of the body, therefore how can you know your Self?

Q: *How can I experience my Self?*

M: Is it because of the body that you do not see your Self?

Q: *Perhaps because "I am".*

M: I am leading you in that direction. You *are*; because you are, your world is. You are lost in the names and titles imprinted on that world. Give up the habit of labelling whatever you are. Be what you were prior to the label or title, be that.

Q: *Is it intuitive, not of the mind?*

M: Don't employ the mind, do nothing.

Q: *Should you not be aware?*

M: That awareness will be there provided you are. You must give up all you have read and heard, and just *be*. Don't be carried away by concepts. Truth is eternal; whatever you can grasp is unreal. Even your experience that you are is not your true nature. You, as the Absolute, are not this "I Amness", but presently you have to abide in your "I Amness".

Q: *I feel afraid.*

M: Because you have assumed something as "I Am", which actually you are not, that is why you are afraid. Suppose you find a diamond ring on the road and you pocket it. Since it is not yours, a fear overcomes you. When you put on an identity that is not yours, you are afraid. When you are the pure "I Amness" only, there is no fear. Presently you are this "I Am", but this "I Am" is not the truth. Whatever you are prior to the appearance of "I Am", that is your true nature.

February 25, 1981

Maharaj: Each one lives in the world according to certain preconceived concepts. Whatever spiritual knowledge he thinks he may have achieved, he continues to live according to those concepts.

Questioner: *What is it like to live with no concepts?*

M: Any answer given to you will be a concept.

Q: *How can one know that he is beyond concepts?*

M: Merely to understand, without the slightest doubt, with great conviction, that there is a state prior to the arising of this consciousness. That, itself is, sufficient.

Q: *How can one differentiate between just having the thought of it and living it?*

M: How do you understand anything? Any knowledge of any kind that you think you have can only be in the consciousness. How can the consciousness, which came later, give you any knowledge about that state which exists prior to its arrival?

Any thought that you have reached or are going to reach that state is false. Whatever happens in consciousness is purely imaginary, an hallucination; therefore, keep in mind the knowledge that it is consciousness in which everything is happening. With that knowledge, be still, do not pursue any other thoughts which arise in consciousness. What is necessary is to understand with sure conviction is that all is temporary, and does not reflect your true state.

February 27, 1981

Questioner: *Could Maharaj speak on the relationship between body and spirit?*

Maharaj: You must get to know your own Self. This body is not your true nature. The principle by which you know "I Am" is your true nature.

Q: *What responsibility do I have towards other people?*

M: You have built your responsibilities around the teachings which you have derived from the world, but what is that "you" which is accepting all the responsibility? You must understand that first. You are identifying yourself as a body; that is not Self-knowledge.

Q: *I don't always feel that I am the body; when I become still and concentrate, I realize that there is more than just flesh and blood there. It is a new realization for me.*

M: Have you come to the conclusion that there is no difference between different groups of people?

Q: *Except that some people are more greedy and ambitious. I like to visit foreign countries, meet various kinds of people with different customs.*

M: Don't roam about; don't come here, either. Abide in quietude, peace, stability. Here we are not engaged in any buying or selling. That knowledge "I Am", without concepts, is evoked or stimulated by the consciousness and peace which emanate from this place.

Q: *That is why it is valuable to be with Maharaj.*

M: I am not able to speak much. Don't ask questions. If you want, you may go elsewhere.

Q: *I have been with Maharaj before and I have felt a profound effect from that visit. I understood more.*

M: Whatever the experiencer feels or thinks is all in the consciousness, and is not real.

Q: *It is difficult for me to express.*

M: There is no individual looking at another individual; the sense of presence is cognizing. Other than that, there is nothing. This state of consciousness cognizing what appears in consciousness is being witnessed as a temporary state. The alternate states of waking, sleeping, and the sense of presence are all temporary states that have come upon me. I am not the states. They have all come spontaneously and will go spontaneously. No one has any control over them. Are any of these states your true nature?

Q: *The sense of presence is what I feel I am.*

M: Will that remain permanently? You must understand that truth is not changeable. Truth is constant and eternal, whereas the combination of these three states has come upon you and were not there earlier. Whatever is temporary and time-bound cannot be the truth.

It is good, as far as it goes, that you have identified with this sense of presence, but understand that even that is temporary and not your true nature.

The most important thing for you is the "I Am". Just be that and the necessary guidance will come.

March 2, 1981

Questioner: *Maharaj has said that he used to think of himself as an individual, but now he does not, for that would be identification with the body. The fact that the body continues even afterward -I mean - the body is so strong that it can continue for a certain period even after one realizes that he is not. Maharaj has said that when this sickness started, the last traces of individuality disappeared.*

Maharaj: What is your question?

Q: *Is the identification with the body so strong - I mean - is it such a habit that one identifies with the body even after one knows what lies beyond?*

M: It is not identification as a person, as you think. The body is an aid for the manifestation of consciousness, for experiencing. So long as this consciousness exists, it needs an instrument; without the body, consciousness cannot exist in that form. What is lost is the feeling of being a separate entity.

A jñani is like an unborn child, the consciousness is the child when it is born, and the child is sick. This material, objective body is sick. The jñani cannot be sick. This body [referring to himself] instrument is disturbed and there is an imbalance; therefore, I am not able to talk properly, nor walk properly.

Only so long as you have a body do you know that you are. This applies to all other creatures also. When the body is, the knowledge "I Am" is also there.

Q: *As the Ultimate, am I not aware of my being?*

M: To the Absolute, the witnessing of this "I Amness" happens.

March 4, 1981

Maharaj: How did you get this "I Amness"? Did it come spontaneously, or did you try for it? As the Absolute, you were free from all concepts, including the primary concept "I Am"; suddenly you were caught up in this "I Amness". Who did it? Has it not happened spontaneously?

Questioner: *Yes, that is true.*

M: You did not have this concept "I Am" in the course of the nine months in the womb. Understand this state of affairs; the concept "I Am" comes spontaneously and goes spontaneously. Amazingly, when it appears, it is accepted as real.All subsequent misconceptions arise from that feeling of reality in the "I Amness." Try to stabilize in that primary concept "I Am", in order to lose that and with it all other concepts. Why am I totally free? Because I have understood the unreality of that "I Am".

I offer my salutations to all the prophets, creeds, religions, etc. I know they are not real, they are only the play of this consciousness. The Truth, the Eternal, cannot be witnessed. It ever prevails.

In your true state there are no words, but you think yourself important and you embrace many words. Poor human beings are caught between worldly life and spiritual life. One in a million understands all this play of consciousness, transcends it.

Q: *What is death?*

M: Death is also a hearsay. Have you experienced death? Having followed the course of spirituality, you have come to the end of personality and there is no more human being. There is only impersonal consciousness. In this realm of consciousness all that is going on is dynamic playfulness, a process of functioning. There is no differentiation in this process as to a person, an entity, a community, a creed, a religion.

In the flash of your consciousness, all this play is going on. The play will come to an end.

March 7, 1981

Questioner: *In pursuing what Maharaj says, the result may be a type of behavior which will be considered peculiar in the world.*

Maharaj: Whose behavior? And considered peculiar by whom? All that IS is the essence of the five elements. By this aperception, the nature of the five elements is not going to change. The essence of the five elements is this momentary sense of presence, as compared to eternity.

You come here with a sense of love and regard for me, and you will benefit to the extent of how you perceive me. If you continue to see me as an individual, that will be the extent of your benefits; if you see me as I see myself, and as I see you, that will be the further measure of your benefits. The real state is that state which was prior to the arrival of consciousness. Very few will have reached that state. Most of you will not want to go beyond identification with an entity or a body.

This identification, which has been changing from infancy to your present state, and which will continue to change in the course of time, is purely seasonal.

You identify with the body on the strength of hearsay. Your parents told you that you were born on a certain date, and that this body is what you are. So, based on hearsay, you formed your identity with a certain image. You may think that now you have become jñanis and that you know your identity very well, but most often this is a case of sensory deception. Whatever your image of yourself, it is nothing but a concept.

Just understand what you are, and carry on your daily life to the best of your ability.

Q: *Is daily puja (worship) being observed here?*

M: Yes. Here the worshipper is the consciousness, and the object of worship is also the consciousness.

March 12, 1981

Questioner: *What arose first, "I Amness" or desire?*

Maharaj: If the "I Amness" is not there, what else can there be? This consciousness is in a state of flux, not stationary. If the power to manifest itself and that knowingness ("I Amness") have not appeared, no identification can take place. When that "I Amness" appears, and is accepted as real, it is conditioned, or confined to a certain identity.

Q: *I have dropped my identity.*

M: Who has dropped it?

Q: *No one has dropped it. It dropped by itself. It was possible to observe the capacity of the brain not to register anything.*

M: If the non-reaction state was possible, consciousness would not arise.

Q: *If consciousness is only the content of consciousness, then that knowledge is dropped.*

M: What is the necessity of its getting dropped? What was not, will not be. That knowledge was not there earlier and is going to disappear.

There have been so many teachings by the various saints who have appeared and disappeared. In these talks here, where are the references to Christ, Rama, Krishna, or others? Do we refer to them in our dialogue?

There have been so many saints, sages, and jñanis, and each one has been enamored of a particular concept that he wanted the world to know about. Ultimately, the different religions were only individual concepts which appealed to the consciousness in a particular individual at a particular time.

Q: *That is why we are here.*

M: When you came, was it not on account of your body-mind? Not only is the body-mind unreal, but this manifest consciousness, this universe, is also unreal. The "I Amness" is dream-like, ephemeral.

Even the feeling of having understood is likely to lead one into a sense of illusion, because the individual thinks he has found something to impart to others, but there is no individual.

It is so easy to get totally lost when juggling words, by attaching too much importance to them. Just remember that the total functioning of the manifest happens through the friction of the five elements and the talking which takes place is a part of the total functioning. There is no question of anyone seeking a particular benefit for himself as an individual teacher.

Man identifies with the gross form, he neither recognizes nor identifies with the manifest consciousness. All the activities go on because of the consciousness, but no one really understands it.

When people come here they have many questions and they think, after a while, they know something, but when they finally know there will be no questions to ask.

March 13, 1981

Maharaj: Everything happens out of our own Self. This consciousness is spontaneously felt in the Self only. This "I" is not an individual. What *is*, is the Absolute unmanifested. What appears, as if in a dream, is the manifested, relative world, and this experience of the dream-like state is the same, an identical state, for everyone.

In this process of functioning that becomes manifest, if you accept something as an individual event then it affects you as an individual. If you do not take delivery as an individual but as total functioning, then you are free of whatever is happening. The knowledge of the Self is this dream-like feeling of "I Amness". By assuming a separate identity one taints that which is taintless; that is the original sin.

Go to the very root: who are you, what are you? You are the product of the five elements, you have taken the support of the five elements. Your feeling of "I Amness" emanates from the five elements. Focus your attention at that point. What change should occur in you so that you realize your Self? What change could happen to you? When you come here, you must be expecting something to happen. What change do you expect in yourself so that you may say, "I have now attained what I sought. I need not go to Maharaj any more." With reference to what state are you speaking? What is that state? In that dream-like state, I am not keeping a record of anyone coming here, nor of any conversations among us.

March 21, 1981

Questioner: *If someone understands the truth, does this have any effect on the world at large?*

Maharaj: The first thing that happens is that the individuality is lost, and whatever happens then is seen as total functioning; the understanding of the total functioning cannot be divided. There is no question of "I" or "you" understanding something. It IS understanding.

This knowledge is not found in books. It is not intellectual knowledge. Although this consciousness functions through millions of forms, it is one and the same consciousness.

We have this conviction that I am, I exist, I'm alive. That conviction is because of the consciousness, and consciousness is not aware of itself unless the body is there, so what is the relationship? Consciousness is the taste of this physical form. If the form is not there, the taste is not there. The body is the essence of food and the consciousness is the essence of the physical form. If this is properly understood, is there any individuality? This individuality is a process of manifestation.

Q: *Why does the consciousness want to preserve itself in a particular form?*

M: When the consciousness identifies itself with a form, it is the nature of this identity to want to continue as long as possible. Consciousness loves that identification so much that it wants to continue.

Q: *If this individuality is lost, will consciousness still want to continue?*

M: Once consciousness has lost its individuality and has become one with the universe, it will have no need to continue?

March 24, 1981

Maharaj: If you sit here quietly, being one with the knowledge "I Am", then you are not concerned with the world or what goes on in the world. It is only when the consciousness starts operating and there are various movements in the consciousness that the behavior in the world takes place. When I am not conscious of the existence of the body, experiences are not registered.

Just as the universe is contained in consciousness, so too this physical body is merely an appearance in consciousness, perceived and cognized by consciousness. No amount of effort can make you understand this; only the deepest apperception of this in consciousness will make that experience happen by itself.

Anyone in that condition, where the consciousness is present but the registration of the existence of the body is not, even in that state the conditions in the body change constantly. All of this is an appearance in consciousness; therefore, consciousness has to suffer all of the changing conditions.

In that state any number of events happen, but all that is really happening is a total functioning against the background of this void which, in reality, is really consciousness. There is no separate identity; what IS is this consciousness, apart from that no one can exist.

When you are very quiet, you have arrived at the basis of everything. That is the deep, dark blue state in which there are millions of stars and planets. When you are in that state, you have no awareness of your existence.

March 29, 1981

Questioner: *If the consciousness in all the different forms is identical, then why do thoughts and actions differ from one human being to another?*

Maharaj: The thoughts and actions belong to the body-mind and the body-mind is the essence of the five elements. The nature of the form depends on the various degrees of the five elements and the three *guna*s. The thoughts and deeds depend on the conditioning received right from the time the consciousness is there. Without the consciousness, there would be only dead forms.

Consciousness and the body are kept in working condition by the food and medicine that we imbibe. In each form the thoughts, words, and deeds depend not only on the conditioning the form has received after it has been created; but they depend on even earlier conditioning at the time of conception. The consciousness was latent in that birth chemical.

How amusing it is that one identifies with the body. How long have you been following spirituality?

Q: *For forty years. I was following the "Who am I" of Ramana Maharshi, and I have read the book of Maharaj's teachings.*

M: So far, so good. What do you understand about your own Self? What are you?

Q: *Consciousness.*

M: The Ultimate is prior to any experience. "I Amness" is the beginning of experience. On the Ultimate there appeared this knowingness, and the question arose, "Who or what am I?" That feeling of being is not colored by form. It is just a feeling of being, of "I Amness". That was the first experience.

Q: *This is Maya.*

M: Because you don't get the answer to "Who am I," you give the reply that this is *Maya*. You cannot catch it by a reply. With what do you identify?

Q: *I am the Brahman.*

M: This is not your direct experience. You are just repeating what you have read or heard. What do you think you are?

Q: *I have experienced....*

M: The experience can be there when the "I Amness" is there, but prior to this experience "I Am", what was the state?

Q: *I do not know.*

M: I am talking to you because you have the wisdom to understand.

Q: *Can I stop this "I Amness" and be before the "I Amness"?*

M: What natural processes can you stop? Everything is spontaneous. Presently you are in the consciousness, which is stirring, vibrant. Don't think you are something separate from this stirring, vibrant consciousness. You are part of the play of this consciousness. You, the consciousness, are the product of the food consumed.

At the level of active consciousness, which is Self, and which is in activity, there cannot be identity of a body

Q: *How can I be convinced of this?*

M: When you remain still in your Self, then you receive the conviction. You stay in quietude.

April 6, 1981

Questioner: *While I am sitting here, putting questions to you, I feel at peace. Is it not a landmark, showing progress?*

Maharaj: What are you talking about? You are talking from the kindergarten level. I am not going to address you as a student of the *mumuksha* class, I am going to address the class of *sadhaka*. How long have you been practicing spirituality?

Q: *Since childhood, because my family has been practicing spirituality for generations; therefore, I have a hobby of spirituality.*

M: Very good. Nevertheless, you are still at the kindergarten level. The only solution is for you to give up your identity with the body-mind.

Q: *I know all of this intellectually, but I am not experiencing it, so I came for satsang.*

M: What do you mean by *satsang*? This is merely a conventional spiritual jargon. Now you go from here with the firm conviction that "I am the *Brahman*, without any shape, form or design, and without any mental inclinations. I am the manifest consciousness." When you realize that you are formless, there is no caste or creed for you, there are no concepts left.

The *mumukshu* is in kindergarten, spirituality inclined, but identifying with the body-mind. The *sadhaka* is one who has dis-identified with the body-mind. A *Siddha* is one who has stabilized in the knowledge "I Am", and in the process, has transcended it. In this journey you know very well where you are.

M: [Speaking to another person] This young man's mother was on her deathbed, but I said with conviction that she was not going to die. This was some years back and today, she is still alive. His mother was so convinced that she was going to die that she had purchased the particular flowers which she liked for her funeral. I ordered her to get up and go and prepare tea for me.

At that time, my attitude was that "I am the *Brahman*"; today that attitude is discarded. I had the firm conviction then that whatever I tackled would take shape, would happen. At this very place many things happened. *Bhajan*s have been going on here since 1932. I was the first tenant in the Vanmali building.

[There was more talk of other miracles which had happened there. There were a lot of miracles that happened around Maharaj, but he never cared to speak about the past or the future.]

M: People would come here hoping to get their problems solved, and when I would ask why they had come, they would simply state their problems. I would tell them, "The very fact that you have come here means that your problem is bound to be solved. You can go." Now all of you are coming; who is drawing you here? It is your own beingness. You are attracted to this place because of a certain quality in you. You are stabilizing in the highest state. It is not a worldly attraction which brings you here. Neither you nor anybody else knows anything about this attraction. The attraction for you is to be in your eternal dwelling place, that is your home. When that attraction is there you come here.

Q: *Scientists have been talking of the "black hole" into which everything in the universe finally goes.*

M: You are that Absolute, you swallow the entire universe.

April 10, 1981

Maharaj: There is only the slightest touch of "I Amness" left. Henceforth, people will be able to have only *darshan*, there is not much chance of talking. Whatever faith you entertain about me, that will stabilize in you. It is not the *darshan*, but your faith in the *darshan*.

Unusual, rare, strange, astonishing, non-phenomenal; this is the kind of benefit you will receive. The ultimate faith in the Self. Total faith. Whatever you see, don't see it as a mere body. These are truly the limbs of that highest, imperceptible principle that is expressing itself. These limbs have reached the highest.

Questioner: *I am convinced.*

M: Now that conviction is so strong for you that it can never be broken. It is total, complete, imperishable.

April 11, 1981

Maharaj: The core of this consciousness is knowingness, to know "I Am". It is not a personality, not an individual. It is total manifestation. Beingness is there, it fills everything.

Nevertheless, this quality "I Am" is the result of the material, objective body. In the seed the whole tree is latent; in the droplet "I Am" all three worlds are squeezed in.

The highest state is the state of a jñani. The first step is to be that droplet. In the process of knowing that droplet, you are out of it, and that is a jñani. A jñani is not obsessed by any calamities or any problems, because he has transcended the "I Am" principle. He watches the play as a witness.

Now, understand clearly. This "droplet" of knowingness is a result of the food essence body; in understanding it, you are out of it. If this last step is taken, knowing that I, the Absolute, am not that "droplet", the consciousness, it has to happen only once. There is no more involvement with the play of the consciousness. You are in a state of no return, the eternal state.

Whatever you think of as spiritual knowledge was gained in the realm of consciousness; such knowledge is merely a burden upon your head and it is going to add more misery.

It is nothing more than spiritual jargon. This "I Amness" is the very source of all misery.

Are you in such a position that you cannot employ any words to express your Self? When I answer your questions at such great length, you should be reduced to a quietude out of which no words can come.

I expound this knowledge completely and thoroughly. Have you the courage to accept it?

If you have really understood what I have told you, you need not come again. Do not try to tell these things to all and sundry, just don't speak of this elsewhere.

April 22, 1981

Maharaj: The whole universe is experienced in the consciousness "I Am". If that is not there, what else can ever exist? This consciousness is beating a drum; everyone is carried away by the noise of the drum. Who looks for the drummer? Who is sounding and beating the drum? It is so amazing that no one casts even a glance at this speck of consciousness.

Questioner: *When I stabilize in consciousness, is that meditation?*

M: Who is stabilizing? Is it not the consciousness itself?

This one [referring to Jean Dunn] has understood her nature. It is all due to her faith in the Guru. Everything that has any concern with me is sacred to her. Unless you have such faith in the Guru, you do not attain faith in your Self. Some people go about to this swami and that swami, for what? To lick at their left-overs. If they lick their own left-overs, how much better it would be.

Stick to your own consciousness, remain in that. All the burden of your concepts you should fuse into your consciousness, but do not use your consciousness to build up the edifices of concepts.

Q: *Habit is a great force which makes one stray, isn't it?*

M: The habit of considering Self as the body has influenced everybody too much. The knowledge "I Am" is your Guru, be in it.

Who is the one who sings the *bhajan* ? It is the intellect of that Guru - who are you, an intruder? Of course, the action of the whole world depends on this intellect, but when this intellect reaches its apex, it gets merged into *Parabrahman*.

You all go on writing a diary of your own concepts - I tell you, finally, it is utterly useless. It will only serve as an instrument of bondage.

June 5, 1981

Maharaj: You now know that you are. How has this happened, because of what do you know that you are? You have to go to the source. One hundred years earlier you did not know your own existence. You had no problems at that time. Now, because of this knowingness, all the problems have started. This "I Amness" has appeared because of the body, so what knowledge do we have about the body and what knowledge of this "I-ness"?

Questioner: *When the body falls, when the person is dead, do the memory and the consciousness remain?*

Maharaj: Both the memory and consciousness are the quality of the food body. When the body is not present, there is no question of their remaining. The "I Amness" is a quality of the food body, but that is not the nature of the true Self.

Q: *What is turiya?*

M: *Turiya* means that only you remain; nothing else remains. So long as you know that you are, everything is. Find out what you are and you will get all the answers; find out the source of the body and the source of this "I Amness". If you find this out, you will know what you are.

Whatever changes is not your Self; this body is continuously changing. It was not there, it appeared and it will disappear. It is not you. Find out what you are.

The important thing is the consciousness. You must give your full attention to the consciousness itself. That is the process of meditation; then all the secrets will be revealed to you by the consciousness. The consciousness likes that Self-love. If you are interested in the consciousness only, you will come to know it. If you are interested in the world, then it means you are not interested in the consciousness. If you are interested only in the consciousness, then the consciousness will unmask all the secrets and then you will know what you are. This "you" will know who you are, but awareness means pure consciousness and there is no "I" there.

Watching yourself, that itself is meditation. To keep only consciousness, without mixing it with anything, that is knowledge without words, that you ARE. Thoughts will be there, but they will be weaker and weaker, so only the feeling of "I Amness" will remain: just consciousness, without any activity. Watching your activities is on a lower level, like watching anger, etc., that is identification with the body-mind.

Q: *Does Maharaj feel his body?*

M: I come to know that everything is through the consciousness. Just as I see you, I look at this body, but I am apart from it. I am not identified with the body.

Consciousness is not male or female, it is like light. Light also means heat. When the temperature goes down, the doctor will say that the patient is no more.

Q: *What about reincarnation?*

M: Even this birth is false. The quality of "I Amness" is because of the body. You don't know whether you exist or not in deep sleep; you don't know you are, that is all. You were not born at all; only the announcement of your existence is there. You existed even prior to your birth; your existence is eternal, but the knowledge that you existed came about when you were a few years old.

Just worry about this birth. Why worry about reincarnation? Think whether this birth is correct.

June 7, 1981

Questioner: *How can one control the mind?*

Maharaj: You accept only good and discard the evil and continuously recite the name of God--that will help you gradually control the mind. What is acceptable to you and gives you peace is good. What your mind rejects is not good. When you do something and there is fear of failure, that means the mind is not pure.

Q: *How does one develop a liking for chanting the mantra?*

M: In the company of the sages you can develop it. From 5:00 P.M. to 6:00 P.M. what goes on? Consciousness comes to meet consciousness. There will be no other talk except some communication between consciousness itself. There will be no other strange third person or individual meddling in there. God has come to meet God. You know that whatever sentiments arise, you are not those.

June 9, 1981

Maharaj: Rajneesh is not a small personality or small principal. He is tremendous - he is very big. He is a great sage.

When you already have a guru [Rajneesh], why do you visit other sages? Since you already have a great sage as your guru, you should not sit here or come here. I do not like those shiftings from gurus to gurus. I do not like wanderers. What is the difference between Maharaj and Rajneesh? Once you remove the letters (that is, the names) what is the difference? You investigate that wanderer's "I", before you investigate others. What is the product after you remove its name. What are you without the name or the label?

You investigate the investigator -- investigate "I Am".

Before you take up the assignment of inquiring about others, inquire about yourself first and see if you are real or unreal. The letters "I Am" are written spontaneously with a certain ink. What is that ink which was used to write that which you are? In that ink with which the letters "I Am" were written, in that ink the title of Tej Sesh Bhagavan is confirmed by the Vedas. Sesh means the leftover, the remains. What is the leftover that means what you are? [Maharaj then asked someone to leave and not to listen to these talks.] One who has understood one's mystery as to what is, that one will not discuss or argue the largeness or smallness of anybody.

You have become a slave to a concept, and having become a slave to one concept you are fully involved and are immersed in more concepts. You are drowning in concepts. Having got caught up with the concept that you are, the first concept, you started giving names and titles and ideas to others and you became enmeshed therein. Although one may call oneself a jñani, one enjoys entertaining himself with a number of concepts. Although such a one knows full well that he is not going to get anywhere, still one becomes busy with a number of concepts. That Taj Sesh Bhagavan has spontaneously come and will spontaneously go. What are you going to get for yourself as "I Am"? In what position or concept did you stabilize yourself as "I Am"? The firm conviction that I am this, the three states --waking state, deep sleep and the knowledge "I Am" -- are the aspects of that Tej Sesh Bhagavan. You are not that.

Question: *Then who am I?*

Maharaj: The prominent and firm reply is only you are. You throw the hooks with bait into the water to catch the fish. In that way you, with the concept that you are, throw in the bait and haul in lots of concepts for yourself. So when the question followed by the answer is there, then anything which is refused (what remains) is that rejection.

Prior to any other recognition, you already are. If you are not, other people are not. You are supporting yourself on the intellect of the body and having stabilized in the body or the intellect, you are creating or inviting a lot of concepts, and in the concepts you are bogged down. You are talking about others, let me know what you are. I am asking about you. What are you? You the observer.

Q: *Maharaj knows I do not know what I am. Why is he asking me?*

M: I am not talking to you. Consciousness is talking to consciousness about consciousness. Who told you that Maharaj is talking to you? Your basis itself is wrong. One appearance noticed another appearance of a fly. That is why this automatic gesture. If I understand what I am, that is, merely an appearance, then I will know the others are appearances also. Therefore, I will have no questions, arguments or quarrels with them. But if I don't understand myself, and if I ride on the wings of a concept, then I prefer my appearance.

Q: *Since Maharaj is only talking to consciousness, he will not talk to my ignorance.*

M: Ignorance will remain there for all time just as knowledge also will remain for all time. There cannot be knowledge without ignorance and there cannot be ignorance without the correlated knowledge. Both are the opposites in manifestation, one cannot remain without the other. Even this concept about knowledge is merely a concept. With a jñani, there is no concept of either ignorance or knowledge. The total absence of all knowledge or ignorance is that state prior to the arising of consciousness. But you try to interpret whatever I say with various concepts and you condition yourself with all these concepts.

Q: *Maharaj is taking everything away from me. I have nothing to hold onto - I will fall.*

M: You will be broken into how many pieces with that fall? With all that, do what you like! Another person is searching for himself, but you are hiding.

Q: *What is reality?*

M: Whatever is permanently there, immortal, unchanging. The eternal ever is, a non-experiential state. Subsequent to that is the consciousness, "I Amness", the body experience and life. Your experiences are in the realm of consciousness. In the realm of consciousness you cannot have the experience of truth. As a matter of fact, there can be no experience of the truth because you are That in the ultimate analysis. How can there be the experience of the truth? It is prior to the beingness.

Q: *What can one do for the continuance of that experience?*

M: No experiences are permanent. You are the permanent. Experiences are there in the realm of consciousness, which is bound by time.

Q: *How does one go beyond time?*

M: How did you come? Experiencing things happens unconsciously or spontaneously. Knowingly you cannot go into that.

Q: *Can we come out of it knowingly?*

M: You want to step out? One must know exactly what is time and what is you. You must get to know that first. What is your step? You want to step out of time. What is time?

Q: *Time is desire.*

M: Not at all, time means space.

Q: *There is separation in space.*

M: Whatever you have placed before Maharaj as knowledge are all mistaken concepts. Do you have the knowledge that birth means misery?

Q: *Pain of birth, not the knowledge.*

M: Just by playing with words and concepts, you will not be emancipated.

Q: *What should one do?*

M: Don't even accept the concept that you have to do anything.

Q: *What should I do with the pain?*

M: The way it has come, it will go.

Q: *Have I to become idle?*

M: Jump about! You understand what I say but you are afraid that whatever so-called knowledge you have collected is being devalued. Krishnamurti said whatever he has said, very rightly, but do you assimilate it thoroughly? Whatever Maharaj tells you, you try to absorb it through concepts.

June 10, 1981

Questioner: *When I meditate I fall asleep. What can I do to overcome that?*

Maharaj: Don't raise this problem at all with me. You are in the three states, the waking state, deep sleep state and the knowledge you are, so why are you dealing with the state which you are not? Why are you interested? It is spontaneously happening. You have to understand that when you are being stabilized in a state prior to waking state, deep sleep, prior to words and even prior to consciousness, something happens in your body state without your doing it. Leave it alone. Don't ask questions about that. You are on this side and if something is happening, why are you worried about it? Be yourself. If you are yourself, you need not worry about what is happening at the other end. You are interested in your experiential state. There are so many experiences; such as, I saw blue light, I went up, etc., don't tell me all those things. Be yourself and not the experiences. This is also a temporary phase and you are giving it undue importance by saying, "Oh, it is something!" It happens naturally.

There was a gentleman who came to me and he told me he would start crying and sobbing for about 10 minutes when he meditated. He thought it was a very great thing that happened to him in the process of Self-realization. What is the point of getting excited and saying, "Oh! I started crying!" So what! You are not the one crying, you are not your emotions, are you? So many people come to Maharaj to tell him of the spiritual experiences which they have undergone through meditation, just to show people, "I am something!"

When you fall into sleep, be alert and remind yourself that "I am the manifest *Brahman*," at that moment, on the borderline. During the course of sleep, your transcendence is prior to mind, and continues during sleep also. If you fall into sleep reciting *japa* and at midnight you wake up, you will find that *japa* continuing. If you are alert, be aware of yourself and you will see light in the deepest recesses of your core.

June 11, 1981

Maharaj: What do you know about your body? What is it and what are you? Body is the form or shape. The taste of the food body is the knowledge "I Am". What is your identity which you feel or experience in this body? Your words are all right but are you the words? You are wearing the clothes - but are you the clothes? There is no permanent form. The body continuously changes. So long as you identify yourself with the body, you will not have satisfaction. This is the space, I am not the space. You must have the firm conviction about your own Self. You must have that deep urge to know yourself. Grace is always there. Your first conviction, that "you are", which is prior to words, to that you have given the form of a body. Give up this bodily identity. Prior to words you are, just be that.

Q: *How can I be that?*

M: Whatever you are, don't give it any shape or design, that is all. If you are, then everything else is. Worshipping books and being devoted to books will lead you nowhere. Be your Self. Be devoted to your Self, worship only that . Worship the knowledge "I Am" as a God, as your guru. Do you see the image of yourself in the mirror first, or do you know you are prior to that? Which is first? If you are not, can you see your image in the mirror? Give up trying to evaluate the real I or the counterfeit I, but associate the I with the *Brahman*, I am the *Brahman*. Whatever you have heard is good enough for you. No further listening to any such knowledge is necessary. Whatever you have listened to so far is good enough for you if you imbibe that and abide in it. Nothing more will be available to you. You are the *Brahman* in totality, nothing more. Unfortunately you have conditioned your Self to believe that you, the *Brahman*, are the body. Now you know you are not the body. Why are you overwhelmed by that counterfeit bodily identity "I"?

You have a lot of knowledge but it pertains to the practical world. So far you have not got the knowledge of the Self. I will not talk about the worldly knowledge. It does not end here.

This is the world. The world is covered by the space. The knowledge of space is there. The space is contained in the knowledge "I Am" and prior to "I Am" is *chidakash*. *Chidakash* ("I Amness") is the source of the universe. *Chidakash* is the root of the mind space. There can't be any knowledge of I am like this or I am like that; you cannot be like this or like that. Because of the *chidakash, mahakash* (the great space) is there. The space of the world is there because of the space of the mind, or prior to mind. One space is covered by more subtle and more expansive space. At the base of that space is the knowledge "I Am". If one abides in the *chidakash* knowledge, one will realize that one has no birth and no death.

June 14, 1981

Questioner: *Continuous daily activity is making the mind dull. I want to know how to make the mind alert.*

Maharaj: I do not speak about the body-mind and what goes on in the world. I talk only about your true nature and your true nature is the sense of presence you have, this consciousness. If you are not conscious, then there is no world for you. There is nothing there. The world exists for you only when you are conscious, so it is about this consciousness, this sense of presence, that I talk.

Once this sense of presence comes, how you act and what you do in the world I don't deal with. This sense of presence, this consciousness, is it not prior to anything else? Even thinking about anything for which you have to use your mind, if you are not conscious, can any thought come? Therefore, this sense of presence, this consciousness, is it not the primary thing without which nothing else can happen? Nothing--no thoughts, no concepts--can arise by themselves. No activity can arise if the sense of presence is not there. The sense of presence does not need any activity of the mind to know that you are present. You do not have to ask yourself, "Am I present, am I conscious?" There is that intuitive sense of presence, you know you are present.

This sense of presence, it is not the sense that I am present, you are present, or any individual is present. The sense of presence is the sense of presence, as such. Because one identifies oneself with his body, he thinks he is born and is going to die. What is born is the general sense of presence, as such. The sense of presence which has come spontaneously will leave spontaneously. There is no individual except through identification with the body. The sense of time, or duration, or the event happening in time, all that can come about only if there is consciousness. If there is no consciousness, do you have the sense of time?

There is the wick and there is the fuel; only then can the light be there. So light depends on the duration of the fuel. That is how the time factor comes in. The sense of presence, this consciousness, is everything. So find out how that arises and how long it is going to last. Just as the light will remain only as long as there is fuel for it, so this consciousness will last only so long as this fuel is there, fuel being the body, which is made of the five elements which are an accumulation of food. If the food is not supplied constantly to the body, the body will not last, and if the body will not last, then the consciousness will not last. Therefore, this consciousness will depend on how long the body is there. Even this consciousness is not everything and it is not going to last for all time. Find out how that consciousness has arisen, the source of the consciousness.

What is this body? The body is only the accumulation of food and water. This food and water are certainly not you, and this consciousness is merely the nature of this food and water. Therefore, you are something separate from either the body or the consciousness. So long as the body is there, anyone who considers himself an individual has as his only capital the sense of presence, this consciousness. Treat that as the highest God and worship nothing else other than the sense of presence, and when you are one with the sense of presence, then whatever is necessary by way of spiritual knowledge will sprout by itself.

If you have any problems or questions with which you are concerned, you will find these problems and questions, are based on your identity with the body and mind as an individual. If that identification is not there, then no questions can arise. You will come to this conclusion.

June 16, 1981

Maharaj: Each one does his own work, but each one has his own quality.

Here are some tests to know whether you are on the spiritual path or not. Investigate what you are thinking of during the twenty-four hour day. You say you got the knowledge of the Self, you have collected the knowledge of the Self; nevertheless, during the whole day what are you discussing inside, in your mind flow? You are discussing all your daily affairs. You don't discuss the way the discussions are going on here about your identity, about what you are; that you don't discuss. Is there anybody who discusses with himself only about the Self? You are according to the quality of the intensity of your thinking.

I also am restless. The type of pain and misery I am now undergoing, nobody else in my place experiences in the world. This talk is not for the consumption of all.

Beyond the realm of consciousness arising from the body, there is no experience of consciousness. I want to talk about that state beyond the realm of consciousness. There are millions of names, but all these names relate to the objective world. Even the title of "parents" is also due to the bodies; as a result of the body this title of "parents" has arisen. I want you to understand clearly that without the bodily consciousness there is no *Brahman*; the *Brahman* is because the consciousness is and consciousness is because the body is. The body consciousness is the result of the five elements. Body consciousness and the world are not different; they are identical. Ponder over this in this fashion.

Whatever is grasped by the mind and intellect is this objective world. Although you have heard these talks, still you will be carried away by your conceptual experiences.

This body is made of food, but what is your true identity? It is something like the body having completely adjusted, like the grains which you have stored being completely adjusted. This is food only. This is the food body and the consciousness. The Absolute is your true identity. I have given you some indication of the Absolute. You have not surpassed the consciousness, and consciousness is the first step. Total consciousness is not the end.

June 18, 1981

Maharaj: People come here because they feel there is a need to come. The consciousness in your body feels pleasure in coming here. So long as consciousness feels the need of anything, you will be compelled to do it. When consciousness leaves, there will be no more bondage.

Other than this sense of presence, which we have because of consciousness, what has anybody got? The real happiness, without its counterpart, can only be there when consciousness leaves. So long as consciousness is there, so long is happiness and unhappiness there. Pure happiness can only be there when consciousness is not there. Whatever can be perceived is totally different from what I am. I have understood my *swarupa* and I am that; it has nothing to do with whatever is manifested.

You can never isolate yourself from the consciousness unless consciousness is pleased with you and gets rid of you. Consciousness opens the gate for you to transcend consciousness.

There are two aspects; one is conceptual, dynamic consciousness which is full of concepts, and the other is transcendent consciousness. Even the concept "I Am" is not there. Conceptual, qualitative *Brahman*, the one that is full of concepts and is qualitative, is the outcome of the functioning body. This consciousness is dead to me; it is gone. I have transcended that. So whatever is, is that other consciousness, that one which is without concepts.

The principle that is conceptual and full of qualities, which I transcended, was like a very big ocean. Now it is mostly dried up, just the dregs remain. Only a very little bit is still there, only a few particles. What is pervading and prevailing is without concept or quality. What remains is talking to you now. Where is the question of birth or death for that remaining principle? You, with your wisdom, are stuck here; you are sticking to certain concepts. If you had no concepts, why should you come here?

You study only those concepts which arise from within you. Those concepts which you do not like will not occur to you. Suppose you do not like mathematics, that subject will not appeal to you; it is a stranger to your concepts. You will be involved with only those subjects or matters which you like. Analyze your thoughts and see if this is not true. Find out the nature of your thoughts. Are they spiritual?

I abide in the state where there is no mind.

June 19, 1981

Maharaj: All happenings are only in body consciousness. Personalities only exist in body consciousness. The usual knowledge is concerned only with the body image. You are not the body, you are the consciousness. There is no imprint of personality, it is the manifest consciousness which is functioning. This dynamic, manifest consciousness is always in a fluid state. What will happen no one can say.

This dynamic consciousness does not have any concept that something good or bad is going to happen to it; it is just happening. No one is doing it.

The message "I Am" is there. The mind-flow is also there; it is not a personality, it is the consciousness. The very idea that you are the body is ridiculous; the consciousness is experiencing its manifestation. A rare being will realize this. The worldly life of a jñani means the total functioning of consciousness. Normally, a person who is always thinking of others as personalities will not think of others simply as a function in consciousness. The play of the consciousness will not come down to an individual level. It is quite different, it is manifestation only.

Are you not a disciple of a great Sage? How many years have you been going to him?

Questioner: *For seven or eight years.*

M: Then why did you come here?

Q: *I wanted to have your darshan, I wanted to meet you.*

M: When you are stabilized in your own Self, then there is no otherness, you are everything. If you abide in your Self you are like space and there is no duality left. You are as expansive and as subtle as the space, and that is liberation. You are not conditioned by any name or form. If you are like space, what is the point of going elsewhere? The space which is here is also everywhere else. Spirituality is not a child's play. My sentences will tear to pieces the doubts of anyone who listens to them. First of all, you abide in your own Self and transcend it, and in transcending, you will realize your Ultimate. The words emanating here are not borrowed knowledge, which is available in scriptures and other books; this is from direct experience. *Nirupana* means the normal practice of these professional spiritual people, they will be expounding knowledge from various books.

You must thoroughly understand what you are, or what you could be when nothing is. When nothing is, you still are. What is that you? It is all one, and when everything is, still you are; that is understandable, but when nothing is, how can I be?

June 21, 1981 A.M.

Maharaj: Any image you have of yourself is not true. True knowledge is to abide in your own Self. Try to understand all this knowledge which you are now gathering. The so-called knowledge you get elsewhere talks only about ignorance; it cannot talk about the Self, true knowledge. All of what is pursued by the mind it is not true knowledge. True knowledge cannot be understood easily. If I had the experience "I Am" before, would I care to enter the womb of my mother? Prior to entering the womb I did not know myself, there was no knowledge of "I Amness". All so-called knowledge is tainted by words, which is only ignorance. You, the Absolute, watch the waking state, you know the consciousness, you know the sleeping state; therefore, you are not that.

Among the millions of people who have come and gone, where am I counted among them? There is no individuality connected with any of those forms, but I have always been, and I am, the total functioning. Without me the functioning cannot take place. I am the total functioning every moment, millions of years ago or now.

In spite of my clearly understanding the foregoing, the bodily suffering has to be undergone because of the consciousness. The name of the consciousness is suffering itself. The life of suffering is nearly over. Whatever this principle is, together with the body and consciousness, it is experiencing all the sufferings and knows itself that it is worth millions of dollars, like a keg of gold. This principle, which has understood and realized what the suffering and the consciousness is, is worth millions. I do not follow the spirituality of the masses. In this place spirituality of the common type will not be doled out to you. That Ultimate you can never be lost; whatever you have lost, you have lost only the words. That Ultimate you knows or feels "I Am" without words. Through this "I Am" comes the world knowledge. You are not in isolation, you are part and parcel of the world knowledge.

Jivatman is the one who identifies with the body-mind as an individual separate from the world. The *Atman* is only beingness, or the consciousness, which is the world. The Ultimate principle which knows this beingness cannot be named at all. It cannot be approached or conditioned by any words. That is the Ultimate state.

I do not want meek and humble disciples, I want them to be powerful, as I am. I do not make disciples, I make Gurus.

I want you to jump in the test tube in the process of this investigation.

June 21, 1981 P.M.

Questioner: *How can I stay stable in awareness?*

Maharaj: You know you are. That itself is awareness. If you think that you have to be aware, then it becomes an experiential state. You want to experience something. Don't recognize your body as yourself. That is all right for your daily worldly affairs, identifying with the body, but when you have to understand yourself, don't understand that you are the body. You have the knowledge "I Am". That itself means you are.

Awareness is that state in which the consciousness subsides into itself.

This body is the expression of the product of the food consumed. Material is consumed in the form of food and this is the result. When the food becomes less and less, the body is bound to become emaciated, become thin. This is not your identity. This is not your image. This is a tiffin box [referring to the body]. Why has this face gone lean? Because the food supply has been reduced. The food body you are not. The waking state you are not. The deep sleep state you are not. You know the waking state. Since you know the waking state you are not the waking state. You know the deep sleep state; therefore, you are not the deep sleep state.

Q: *I am lost.*

M: That Ultimate "you" can never be lost. Whatever you have lost, you have lost only the words. Who told you that you are lost? You know you are, "I Am".

The moment the feeling "I Am" appears, the world also appears. "You are" is not alone, in isolation. You are part and parcel of the world knowledge.

In the consciousness hierarchy there are three stages:
1. *Jivatman* is the one who identifies himself with the body-mind. One who thinks I am a body, a personality, an individual apart from the world. He excludes and isolates himself from the world as a separate personality because of identification with the body and the mind.
2. Next only the beingness, or the consciousness, which is the world. "I Am" means my whole world. Just being and the world. Together with the beingness the world is also felt - that is *Atman*.
3. The Ultimate principle that knows this beingness cannot be termed at all. It cannot be approached or conditioned by any words. That is the Ultimate state.

The hierarchy I explain in common words, like: I have a grandson (that is *jivatma*). I have a son and I am the grandfather. Grandfather is the source of the son and grandson.

The three stages cannot be termed as knowledge. The term knowledge comes at beingness level. I have passed on to you the essence of my teachings.

With what identity do you recognize yourself now? With what identity did you come into this world? With what identity would you like to quit this world? Normally people cling to this bodily identity but now I have thrown overboard this identity - you are not the body. I am asking "What are you? What would be your identity now, since you are not the body? Whatever you would say in words would be incorrect, would be wrong.

You are tenaciously clinging to the body as yourself. You must have a firm conviction that you are not the body, and not even the consciousness in the beingness.

Experiment upon yourself. You are witnessing the stick and are you telling the stick that "I am witnessing you?"

Nothing is useful, no talk is useful when one is by one self. When one subsides in one's true identity, nothing matters, because nothing is. When "I" subsides, it's all awareness.

June 22, 1981 A.M.

Maharaj: This consciousness and "I Amness" are due to what? What is the basic material necessary for that to sprout? It is the five elements, three *gunas*, and *prakriti-purusha.* All those result in this space "I Am". What do you have except memory? The memory is the result of the five elements and three *gunas*, the eight-aspects. So when that basic material is available, only then is memory there- memory of anything, and finally, most important, the memory that you are.

Presently, the feeling that you are is also a memory. To sustain that memory of "I Am", all these raw materials are necessary. You are not that "I Am". You are, as the Absolute, prior to this "I Am". This "I Amness" is the product of these raw materials, but you, as Absolute, are not that. At the most you might say "I Am", but what is this "I Am"? "I" is merely a word. In the first instance, there are words and then there is merely a memory. Memory you are not. Who has been able to retain his memory as "I Am"? Once all that raw material has gone, where is that memory "I Am"?

Your most essential step is to stand firmly on your identity as the dynamic, manifest consciousness principle. You stabilize only here. This is your first step. There is nothing else but the knowledge that you are, just be that. Nothing more, nothing less.

One cannot see rays of light, as such, they reflect only when they encouter another object. Similarly, "I Amness" is the interruption because of these five elements and three *gunas*. That is why the feeling "I Am" is felt; but without the feeling of "I Am", still you are. Light itself emnates from the sun. Everything is stored, the five elements are there; therefore, it is reflecting as the sun. Brightness is seen as the sun because something is there; if something were not there, the rays of light would be spread all over and become invisible as a source of light.

Mahakash is the infinite space. The infinite space is dark. It is as dark as when you close your eyes. In that physical space all the universe arises and sets and is destroyed.

Finally, what is the result of all the experiences that are going on in the play of consciousness? They are just gone, ending up in pure space.

The whole world is in an ever-changing state. No form will remain permanently. Finally all the forms will vanish in space and become formless.

I am talking directly from my own experience, not from any books.

Millions of people, animals and other beings have come and gone. But the sum total of the universe--has it become more or less? It remains unchanged. has They have never become less. They are always there.

With all these millions of forms in the world, can "my" image be left permanently? Presently you have only the feeling of "I Amness" and because of that feeling the whole world is manifested.

Once the millions of people have gone, what traces are left of them? Let us forget spirituality for the time being. Among all of my experiences, I had occasions for joy, happiness and miseries. What part of the miseries or happiness still remains. One who has transcended the consciousness, or one who has seen the end of this, for such a one, where is there the question of any gain or loss?

I know full well that this knowingness will not remain. I abide in that no-knowing state. So, this being the case, where is the question of one's engaging in activity? With such a spiritual orientation, can one be affected by worldly or family life?

June 22, 1981 P.M.

Maharaj: Both experience and experiencer will disappear. I will not elaborate further. Changes get expressed in the consciousness and so consciousness becomes subtler and subtler. Forms get dissolved. The first step on the road to spirituality is to develop that conviction that I am not the male or the female.

Looking outside for light and sound, all disciples undergo some spiritual experience and that itself is bondage. They compare their experiences with others. Those disciples think they are very advanced. They are attracted to the experiences of sound and light, etc., because they identify themselves with the body. They want a shape and design; therefore, they revel in experiences which indicate shape and design.

You should be like space. If you pay attention to things external to you, you will be carried away. If you are the space and not the body, then at that stage the body does not remain as the body because there is nobody to evaluate the body as body. In *chidakash* you evaluate the world as name and form, but when name and form are dissolved, a dissolution takes place. All forms dissolve in *mahakash*. You evaluate a form, that it is like this or like that. When evaluation is not there, the mind is not there, it is like space.

Chidakash is that raw material by which you evaluate whatever you experience or whatever you observe. In the process of becoming more subtle, the external forms are dissolved into *mahakash*; no more names and forms. Simultaneously, the process of evaluation and mind functioning stops, dissolves itself into *chidakash*. When both *mahakash* and *chidakash* become still, it is space only and you are the space.

Because of the external body, the "I Amness" is felt. However, in the absence of the body, the "I Amness" is still there without feeling "I Am". I am ever-prevailing.

June 23, 1981

Maharaj: Just as you are not the clothes that you wear, similarly you are not this body. This is the most important step. You will slowly realize you are just like space, because space is the beginning and the end of everything. Suppose you are sick: you want to know all about your sickness, the more serious the sickness, the more you would like to know about it. Similarly, this "I Amness" is also like a sickness. Now you must begin to collect knowledge about that.

Questioner: *How do you begin?*

M: Start with the body. From the body you get the knowledge of "I Am". In this process you become more and more subtle. When you are in a position to witness the knowledge "I Am", you have reached the highest. In this way you must try to understand, and the seeds of knowledge will sprout in you.

When you come to the end of material world-knowledge, at that stage you transcend the observer and the observed.

That means that you are in a true state of beingness. Thereafter you enter the state of transcending beingness, where the identities of the observer and observed disappear.

Suppose somebody abuses you and you find out who it is. Is it the body? It is not the body. Then what could it be? Finally you come to the conclusion that it is spontaneously happening out of whatever that body is. You will not attribute it to any individual. When your individuality is dissolved, you will not see individuals anywhere, it is just a functioning in consciousness. If it clicks in you, it is very easy to understand. If it does not, it is most difficult. It is very profound and very simple, if understood right. What I am saying is not the general run of common spiritual knowledge.

When you reach a state when body is transcended, mind is transcended and consciousness is also transcended; from then on all is merely happening out of consciousness, which is the outcome of the body, and there is no authority or doership. When a sound is emanating out of a body, it is not that somebody is talking, it is just words emanating, just happening, not doing. If you understand the basis thoroughly, it will lead you very far, deep into spirituality.

The Absolute alone prevails. There is nothing but the Absolute. The unmanifest manifested itself, that manifest state is Guru and it is universal.

Who is the one who recognizes this body-mind? This "I Amness" which recognizes the body-mind is without name and form, it is already there.

June 25, 1981

Maharaj: I am inspired to talk but I have no energy. But whatever I say will be so profound that very few people will understand. To start with, everything happens in the space of the cosmos, and it results in concrete actions of the worldly space. All this happens spontaneously. There is no author or doership there.

At world level, various bodies are formed and at body level, we encounter the attraction of the body; first of all our own body, then attraction of the other bodies. Whatever happens in this concrete world, the instruments and the aids come from the space. The raw material comes from the space. The space is there prior to the light. When the light is collected together, it reflects as the sun. Since all this is difficult to understand, the best course suggested is to do *bhajan*!

Determination of good or bad is made only through words. Words, or sounds, are expressions of the space. Only at word level does one think something good or bad will happen; when one identifies with the space, it is the end of good and bad. First of all you identify something as being good or bad for yourself. Then, in an effort to acquire good or to get rid of the bad, you have invented a God - then you worship such a God and do *bhajan* and you pray to that God for something good to happen to you.

June 27, 1981

Questioner: *What is meditation?*

Maharaj: To be one with THAT because of which we know we exist is meditation. There are a number of names which have been given to Gods. All of them represent the same thing -- they represent this knowledge that one is, this beingness, consciousness. This knowledge does not refer to an individual, but to the sense of presence as a whole.

Instead of accepting this knowledge as a total functioning, one wants to cut up the knowledge into bits and pieces, taking a part for himself, based on some concept. Any knowledge based on a concept is not true knowledge.

There is no such thing as an entity. Now you know that you are awake because, you are here and you have that knowledge. There is nothing else other than this knowledge, no entity.

When you are dwelling in this consciousness you see that you are not doing anything, it is all happening spontaneously. There is no question of your trying to do anything. You cannot try to be your Self, because you are your Self.

Q: *I am concerned about my family. I want them to have spiritual propensities and get awakened spiritually. I try to feed them this knowledge.*

M: If they are deserving, whatever has been fed will be received by them.

June 28, 1981

Maharaj: The sprouting of *Aham Brahmasmi* takes place at some subtle place and when it grows, it grows continuously. What is the meaning of this sprouting? It indicates that I am the *Brahman*; then the inspiration, the intuition, begins. The deeper meaning of *Aham Brahmasmi* means an intuitive, inspirational growth from inside, the firm conviction that I am the *Brahman*. Such a one in whom this growth of *Aham Brahmasmi* starts might undergo sufferings, but that one will not lose his understanding or this sprouting of *Aham Brahmasmi*. That is firmly rooted.

"*Aham Brahmasmi*" means that "I am the *Brahman*", but

before saying "I am the *Brahman*", you are already one with *Brahman*, then only will you be able to say "I am the *Brahman*". It is just like the waking state. After awakening, you might say, "I woke up." So the waking state precedes your saying "I woke up."

There are two ways of receiving the knowledge. One way is you are taught the knowledge, you receive it externally. Another way is, the knowledge grows from inside, intuitively.

So far, have you understood your Self by your Self? You have not yet seen your Self, so how can you be convinced of what you are? Whatever you are identifying yourself with at the moment is only the body and the intellect in your body.

Questioner: *One has to use the intellect to understand. I have been reading a lot. Maybe it will take some time to try to develop a deeper emotional understanding?*

M: To understand what you are, and ultimately to identify with the Self that you are, you must meet someone who has identified himself with the Self and also who has understood the Self thoroughly. Have you come across that identity of yours?

Q: *No. I have seen it in other people. That impels one to try to find it in oneself.*

M: When you look at others, that other person is just food essence, as yourself. What more understanding do you have? What is the quintessence of what you are, the inner core of you?

When you people come here, you feel very satisfied and contented. Why? You feel like that because when you are here, you are under the shade of, or you abide in, your own consciousness. That means you are in a state which transcends body-mind and intellect. Since you are in that state, you do not have any form, you do not have any doubts; therefore, you are in that satisfied state. In that state, whatever sentences you hear will be implanted deeply in you and will not be forgotten. There is no way for you to forget those sentences because they lead you to your Self. What you hear, you will not forget when you leave. Abide in this state of shade, in the Self, in the consciousness that you are, even when you go out. Here there is no room for the intellect to play about. Since you do not identify yourself with any form, mind has no avenue for any propagation; the mind subsides in the consciousness. This is space-like, a shade-like state.

Q: *If you are in that state of beingness, is it necessary to say one's mantra?*

M: Suppose you are a woman and you have not been accepting yourself as a woman, so you are told you are a woman. This is the *mantra* "I am a woman, I am a woman." When you are convinced you are a woman, are you going to repeat, "I am a woman, I am a woman"? When you are THAT there is no question of choice. Choice is at the level of body-mind, whether to say the *mantra* or not to say it.

Q: *When consciousness begins to become aware of itself one would logically think that it would merge in itself. But so often it slips back into identifying itself with the body. Why?*

M: Why should consciousness, which is inadequacy, which is sickness, be there at all? To a jñani, consciousness has not happened at all. If the consciousness tries to understand itself, it gets stabilized in due course in the Absolute. And when the consciousness gets stabilized in the Absolute, it knows it is like a ghost, it is not real. It is not palpable.

You did not know your own existence after you were born. Nine months in the womb and for sometime afterwards that "I am so and so" is absent. When you start recognizing your mother, then you also come to be aware of your own existence. That "I Amness" comes sometime later. Mother teaches you, in ignorance, that you are the body and you begin to believe that. Your mind also starts slowly to develop. So right from the beginning, because of ignorance, the Absolute does not know itself; and because of the body, it started knowing that it is--I AM. Because of the ignorance, you had to ask somebody "who am I?" otherwise, you would not have asked anybody. Even so-called incarnations such as Rama were like this, they had to be taught. The incarnations are just like you. The bondage with the body came because of wrong teaching, and then the guru came and told you that you are not the body, and then you were liberated. That is why all these births are taking place. If you knew of the bondage, you would refuse the birth. But because the "I Amness" is absent, you are trapped. Because the "I Amness" is a quality of the body, later on you come to know you are and that you are trapped. But once you know, you are liberated.

June 30, 1981

Maharaj: All knowledge is like the son of a barren woman.

Presently there are only beingness and the functioning. The individuality and personality are thrown overboard. There is no personality, so there is no question of birth, life, or death.

What remains is only the consciousness without name or form. There is no individuality at all. The form needs a name, but when both are not there, then the consciousness remains only so long as the body is there, but without any individuality. The body is of as much use now as it was prior to the birth and after the death. How do you know me? You know me only on the acquisition of body form, name and form. Do you really see me as I am? I doubt it.

Now the conclusion is that the unborn is enjoying the birth-principle. That principle that is born took so much time to understand this, and it is the unborn only which prevails. It took so much time for the Self to understand the Self.

We have tied around our necks so many concepts; death, this "I Am", etc. Similarly, concepts of good and evil are unnecessary. We have developed these concepts and are caught in them.

How does one think about the Self knowledge? Do you abide in the Self or in the process do you think of something else as the Self? You are wrapped up and lost in your concepts.

For instance, you have a concept about friendship. How long do you keep your friends? You keep them so long as they are useful to you. So long as a friend is of some benefit to you, that's how long you would like to keep that friendship. Now, how can I actually derive benefit out of a friend? I, as an individual, am not there, so how can there be a question of benefit? Benefit to whom? How can there be a question of friendship at all.

Anybody who comes here can sit. I will allow him to sit for some time, but later on I will say, "You may leave." Why? Because I have no intention or purpose of having any friendship with that person.

Ordinarily, there is some purpose for deriving certain benefits out of an association with another. When you meet someone in friendship, there may be some intention to serve one another. But I have no friends. Even this "I Amness" will not remain as my friend.

I am not able to talk any longer--the spirit is willing but the flesh is weak. Previously I used to welcome people but now I am not in a position to welcome them. They come, they sit and they go by themselves. I cannot even extend my hospitality.

All my knowledge has gone into liquidation. I am unconcerned.

GLOSSARY

Advaita: Non-duality.
Adya: Primordial, original.
Agni: Fire.
Aham: I, the ego.
Ajñana: Ignorance.
Akasha: Space, the ether.
Ananda: Bliss, happiness, joy.
Arati: Divine service performed in early morning or at dusk.
Asana: Posture, seat.
Ashram: Hermitage.
Atman: The Self.
Avatar: Divine incarnation.
Bhagavan: God, the Lord.
Bhajan: Worship.
Bhakta: Devotee.
Bhakti: Devotion.
Bija: Seed, source.
Brahman: God as creator.
Brahmarandhra: Opening in the crown of the head, fontanelle.
Buddhi: Intellect.
Chaitanya: Consciousness.
Chakra: Plexus.
Chakrapani: Shakti, energy.
Chidakash: Consciousness, space, "I Amness".
Chit: Universal consciousness.
Chitta: Mind stuff.
Deva: Divine Being.
Dhyana: Meditation, contemplation.

Gayatri: Sacred Vedic mantra.

Gita: Song.

Guna: Attribute, quality born of nature. The three gunas are Sattwa, Rajas and Tamas.

Guru: Teacher, preceptor.

Hatha Yoga: Yoga system for gaining control of the physical body and breath.

Hiranyagarbha: Cosmic intelligence, cosmic mind, cosmic egg.

Isvara or Iswara: God.

Jagat: World.

Jagrat: Waking condition.

Japa: Repetition of a mantra.

Jiva: Individual soul.

Jñana: Knowledge.

Kalpana: Imagination of the mind.

Kama: Desire, lust.

Karma: Action.

Karta: Doer.

Kosa: Sheath.

Kriya: Physical action.

Kumbhaka: Retention of breath.

Kundalini: Primordial cosmic energy.

Laya: Dissolution, merging.

Lila: Sport, play.

Linga: Symbol.

Maha: Great.

Mahakash: The great space.

Mahesvara: Great Lord.

Manana: Constant thinking, reflection, meditation.

Manas: The thinking faculty, mind.

Manolaya: Involution and dissolution of the mind into its cause.

Mantra: Sacred syllable or word or set of words.

Maya: Veiling and projecting power, the illusive power of
  Brahman.
Moksha or Mukti: Liberation, release.
Mouna: Silence.
Mula: Origin, root.
Mumukshu: Seeker after liberation.
Muni: A sage, an austere person.
Murti: Idol.
Nama: Name.
Namarupa: Name and form, the nature of the world.
Neti-neti: "Not this, not this," negating all names and forms
  in order to arrive at the underlying truth.
Nirguna: Without attributes.
Nirgunabrahman: The impersonal, attributeless Absolute.
Nirvana: Liberation, final emancipation.
Niskama: Without desire.
Para: Supreme, other.
Parabrahman: The Supreme Absolute.
Prajna: Consciousness, awareness.
Prakriti: Original, uncaused cause of phenomenal existence.
Pralaya: Complete merging.
Prana: Vital energy, life breath.
Prema: Divine love.
Puja: Worship.
Purna: Full, complete, infinite.
Purusha: The Self which abides in the heart of all things.
Rajas: Passion, restlessness, one of the three aspects of
  cosmic energy or gunas.
Sadhaka: Spiritual aspirant.
Sadhana: Spiritual practice.
Sadhu: Pious or righteous person.
Saguna Brahman: The Absolute conceived of as endowed
  with qualities.
Sakti or Shakti: Power, energy, force.

Samadhi: Oneness, when the self merges into the Self.

Samsara: The worldly life.

Samskara: Mental impression.

Sankalpa: Thought, desire, imagination.

Sat-Chit-Ananda: Existence-Knowledge-Bliss.

Sat-Guru: Inner Self.

Satsang: Association with the wise.

Sattva or Sattwa: Light, purity, being, existence, one of the three gunas.

Shastra: Scripture.

Siddha: A perfected being.

Siddhi: Psychic power.

Sloka: Sacred verse.

Sphurna: Throbbing or breaking, bursting forth, vibration.

Sunya: Void.

Sutra: A terse sentence.

Swarupa: Essence, essential nature, true nature of being.

Tamas: Ignorance, darkness, one of the three gunas.

Tattva: Element, essence.

Turiya: Superconscious state, samadhi.

Upanishad: Knowledge portion of the Vedas.

Vac or Vak: Speech.

Vaikuntha: The abode of Lord Vishnu.

Vairagya: Indifference toward all worldly things.

Vasana: Subtle desire.

Veda: A scripture of the Hindus.

Vedanta: The end portion of the Vedas.

Vichara: Inquiry into the nature of the Self.

Vijñana: Principle of pure intelligence.

Virat: Macrocosm, the physical world.

Viveka: Discrimination between the real and the unreal.

Vritti: Thought wave, mental modification.

Yoga: Union, philosophy of Patanjali.

Yogi: One who practices Yoga.